Changing Problem Behavior
in Schools

Alex Molnar
Barbara Lindquist

Changing Problem Behavior in Schools

 Jossey-Bass Publishers

San Francisco • London • 1989

CHANGING PROBLEM BEHAVIOR IN SCHOOLS
by Alex Molnar and Barbara Lindquist

Copyright © 1989 by: Jossey-Bass Inc., Publishers
350 Sansome Street
San Francisco, California 94104

&

Jossey-Bass Limited
28 Banner Street
London EC1Y 8QE

Library of Congress Cataloging-in-Publication Data

Molnar, Alex.
  Changing problem behavior in schools.

  (A Joint publication in the Jossey-Bass social and
behavioral science series and the Jossey-Bass education
series)
  Bibliography: p.
  Includes index.
  1. Behavior disorders in children. 2. Problem
children—Education. 3. Behavior modification.
I. Lindquist, Barbara. II. Title. III. Series:
The Jossey-Bass social and behavioral science series.
IV. Series: Jossey-Bass education series. [DNLM:
1. Behavior Therapy—methods. 2. Child Behavior
Disorders—therapy. 3. Schools. 4. Teaching.

WS 350.6 M727c]
LC4801.M55   1989   371.93   88-31388
ISBN 1-55542-134-2

Manufactured in the United States of America

The paper in this book meets the guidelines for
permanence and durability of the Committee on
Production Guidelines for Book Longevity of the
Council on Library Resources.

JACKET DESIGN BY WILLI BAUM

FIRST EDITION

Code 8907

A joint publication in

The Jossey-Bass

Social and Behavioral Science Series

and

The Jossey-Bass Education Series

Psychoeducational Interventions:

Guidebooks for School Practitioners

Charles A. Maher, Joseph E. Zins

Consulting Editors

*To all those teachers, school psychologists,
school counselors, school social workers,
and school administrators who were willing
to try something different*

Contents

Contents

Organization Man • Case Example: The Relapse
Agreement • Review of the Essentials of
Predicting a Relapse

11. If at First You Don't Succeed: Guidelines
for Trying Again

12. Refining Your Skills in Solving Problems and
Changing Behavior
Putting Your Perspective in Perspective •
Analyzing Your Capacity • Getting Started and
Keeping Going • Develop a Plan • Involve
Others as Consultants to Encourage Your Creativity
• What We Have Learned from Our Students

Resource: Practicing Behavior Change Strategies

References
Index

156

160

172

179
187

Preface

Most teachers, school psychologists, school counselors, school social workers, and school administrators are successful at what they do in classrooms and schools most of the time. However, at one time or another, even the most successful people find themselves "stumped" by a chronic problem, such as children who repeatedly fail to do homework, who are consistently tardy, or who often fight with other children. Although these problems are often not dramatic, they steadily wear people down and undermine school effectiveness. We have written *Changing Problem Behavior In Schools* to help you get "unstuck" when you find yourself struggling with a chronic problem.

   Our book is intended to provide you with an opportunity to examine and constructively rethink your commensense ideas about problem behavior. The ideas we discuss may at first seem unusual. That is what many of the hundreds of experienced teachers, school psychologists, counselors, social workers, and administrators who have taken our "Making Schools Work" course at the University of Wisconsin, Milwaukee or who have attended one of our workshops have told us. Nevertheless, our students have used the ideas described in this book in city, suburban, and rural schools, and they have used them with children of all ages, children of varying ability, and children from diverse backgrounds. However skeptical they may have been initially, once our students tried the techniques we taught them in their own schools and classrooms they found that, more often than not, problem situations were changed for the better.

Sometimes these changes seemed to occur instantaneously, as if by magic; at other times the changes occurred after weeks or even months of persistent effort. Our focus in *Changing Problem Behavior in Schools* is how ecosystemic ideas can be used to promote change. Our orientation toward change has been strongly influenced by the work of family therapists who, drawing on diverse sources such as cybernetics, system theory, and hypnosis, have evolved a body of practical knowledge about how to help people solve their problems. Since ecosystemic ideas are intended to help change problem situations instead of to diagnose or "treat" a particular type of problem, they can be used in a large number of very different problem situations in schools. For example, ecosystemic techniques have been used to solve problems involving very active children, students who sleep in class, administrators who do not involve faculty members in decision making, students who do not do their homework, students who often fight with other students, teachers who make inappropriate referrals, parents who do not come to parent-teacher conferences, students who do not follow instructions, and so on.

Despite the variety of problem situations in which these ideas have been used, educators tend to describe their experience of the problem in characteristic ways. To some, the chronic problem they faced was like a stubborn knot in a shoelace: the harder they pulled and tugged at it, the tighter the knot became. To others, the problem was like holding their hand in front of their eyes: although they knew that there was a good deal more to be seen and taken into account, all they could see clearly was their palm. To still others, it was like struggling in quicksand: the more fiercely they struggled, the deeper they sank. If any of these metaphors captures your experience with a problem you are having, it may be a good time to consider using the ideas in this book.

We call the approach to problem behavior described in *Changing Problem Behavior in Schools* an ecosystemic approach because we view problem behavior as a part of, not separate from, the social setting within which it occurs. In other words, classroom behaviors influence school behaviors and vice versa. Regarding schools and classrooms as ecosystems means that the behavior of everyone in a classroom or school in which a problem occurs influences and is influenced by that problem behavior. From this perspective a change in the perception or behavior of anyone associated with a problem has the potential to influence the problem behavior. We believe this is a very hopeful point of view because it says that everyone in a problem situation has the capacity to influence it positively. The ecosystemic approach has a number of distinctive characteristics:

1. It focuses directly on change in the problem situation rather than on the diagnosis of problem individuals.
2. It does not require elaborate or exhaustive plans either to replace or to supplement current practice. The ideas can be readily and comfortably employed by educators who have different styles and work in a variety of settings.
3. It enables educators to start small with manageable aspects of problems.
4. It encourages divergent explanations for problem behavior.
5. It encourages lightheartedness and open-mindedness in the face of chronic problems.
6. It is designed to build on strengths, not to overcome deficits.
7. The ideas can be mastered without any specialized background knowledge.

In school, problems are characteristically described in terms of individuals, deficiencies, and past events. For example, an adolescent boy or girl who is often aggressive and sarcastic will tend to (1) be identified as the person with the problem, (2) be assessed as having one of any number of deficiencies (attention deficit disorder, hyperactivity, learning disability, and so on), and/or (3) have events and circumstances from his or her past (for example, coming from a broken home) used to explain the aggression and sarcasm. Explaining a problem in this way has several negative consequences. First, although much of what might be said about the child may be true, it is often unhelpful as a guide to positive change. The information does not give much practical guidance about changing the problem behavior. Second, the educator is denied the opportunity to do something about the problem. After all, how can the educator alter a child's personality or events that occurred years in the past? Third, attention is directed away from the social interactions in the school and classroom (of which the child's aggressive and sarcastic behaviors are only one part). Finally, focusing on the behavior of one individual who is regarded as having deficiencies in a problem situation virtually precludes consideration of what the individual does well, what is right with the school and classroom, and what can be changed in the present to make things better.

From an ecosystemic perspective, problems are not seen as the result of one person's deficiencies or inadequacies. Instead, problems are viewed as part of a pattern of interpersonal interaction. Viewed this way, attempted solutions to problem behavior that do not change things for the better are part of the problem. Approaching school problems ecosystemically will, therefore, help you to see problems within their interpersonal contexts and to change your responses in chronic problem situations. We think you will find it a positive and hopeful approach.

Overview of the Contents

Changing Problem Behavior in Schools is divided into three parts. Part One describes the ecosystemic framework we use to explain problem behavior.

In Chapter One we analyze how social, personal, and professional factors influence individuals' perceptions of events and contribute to keeping their behavior in problem situations from changing. The significance of the meanings individuals assign to behavior and the influence these meanings have in maintaining problems is also discussed.

Chapter Two describes the usefulness of the concept of ecosystem and explains how problems and solutions are viewed from an ecosystemic perspective. The importance of a cooperative view of problem behavior is also discussed.

The focus of Chapter Three is how to recognize and use ecosystemic "clues" to help develop the flexible approach to problem solving that will be used with the techniques described in Part Two. Readers are asked to adopt the characteristics of sleuths as they "track down" solutions.

Part Two presents ecosystemic methods for promoting change in problem situations. Chapters Four through Nine are each devoted to a different ecosystemic technique.

The numerous case examples we use to illustrate ecosystemic methods are the heart of Part Two. Each case example is based on one of over two hundred cases described by students in our "Making Schools Work" course over the past six years. We have rewritten the case material for clarity and to provide a more-or-less standard presentation format. We have also changed the names of the people involved; removed all descriptions that might identify a particular educator, parent, student, classroom, or school; and given each case example a name. Our case examples have an unmistakable air of reality about them, because they are based on real events. However, any resemblance a case example may have to an actual person, classroom, or school is purely coincidental.

Each chapter in Part Two follows the same format. The technique is described, case examples are presented and discussed, and the essential elements of the technique are reviewed.

Most of our case examples involve teachers and students. There are, however, also case examples involving school psychologists, counselors, teacher aides, parents, a special education coordinator, a department chair, a learning center director, and so on. This case material is therefore sure to be of interest not only to teachers but also to anyone whose job it is to help solve problems in an educational setting and who feels stuck in a chronic problem situation from time to time.

Part Three is intended to encourage you to implement what you learned in Parts One and Two. Chapter Ten will help you figure out the next step when you try an ecosystemic technique and it works. If you tried a technique and were unsuccessful, Chapter Eleven offers advice about considering what may have gone wrong and how to go about trying again. Chapter Twelve discusses strategies you can use to build on the successes you have had using ecosystemic ideas. The emphasis is on identifying personal and institutional strengths that can be used as a basis for the ongoing implementation of an ecosystemic approach in your classroom and school.

A resource section has been included at the end of the book.

This section contains a practice activity for each of the techniques described in Part Two. The purpose of these practice activities is to help you apply the technique you have selected to a problem in your school or classroom. In each practice activity we help you to think about and to describe your problem in a way that will make it easier for you to use the technique you have selected.

How to Use This Book

Throughout the book we have used an informal, conversational writing style. We have done so because we want (to the extent it is ever possible to do so on a printed page) to talk directly to you. We did not want our ideas mediated by technical terms and formal language. We want you to *use* our book. Read it straight through from cover to cover, pick it up, try an idea, refer back to it, and read some more; use it in the way that is most comfortable for your style and circumstance. We want *Changing Problem Behavior in Schools* to be a useful resource for you.

We expect you to approach the ideas in this book with caution and healthy skepticism. It is true that these ideas have much wider currency in the practice of family therapy than among education professionals. It is also true that the relationship between a therapist and a family is different than the relationship between, for example, a teacher and a class. Therefore, there can be no substitute for your considered judgment in determining if, when, and how to try any of the techniques explained in this book.

Interestingly, as our students have taught us, educators have an important advantage over family therapists in using ecosystemic ideas. A family therapist is, in most instances, hired directly by the family. It is the family who determine what problem they want to solve and what represents an acceptable solution. It is not the therapist's role to tell the family what problem they should want to solve or to attempt to impose a solution on them. In school, however, an educator is in effect a "family" member and as such has the standing to assert that a problem exists and the right to help determine what an acceptable solution will be.

As you read *Changing Problem Behavior in Schools,* it may help you to keep our ideas in perspective if you think of your classroom or school as an ocean liner setting out from Europe for the United States. The ocean liner may need assistance to get safely in and out of harbor or, in extraordinary circumstances, to survive stormy seas. However, harbor pilots and rescue vessels do not determine the ocean liner's ultimate destination. The ideas in this book are like the harbor pilots or rescue vessels in the metaphor. They cannot provide you with a destination, but they can help you effectively navigate the "straits" and the "rough seas" that are a part of life in schools.

Acknowledgments

The ideas in *Changing Problem Behavior in Schools* have been influenced by the work of Steve de Shazer and the team at the Brief Family Therapy Center in Milwaukee, Wisconsin, during the early 1980s. We recognize our debt to them. We would like to thank our friends Judith Jaynes and Raymond Wlodkowski for their unflagging enthusiasm for our ideas and their always well-timed pushing, prodding, and cajoling to get on with our writing. We also want to acknowledge Jane Schneider, who gave us the benefit of a teacher's thoughtful reading of and comment on our manuscript, and Cathy Mae Nelson for her patience, good humor, and competence in typing it. Finally, we want to express our gratitude to our children, Alex, Christopher, Shannon, Heather, and Cavan, for giving us so many opportunities to practice what we preach.

Milwaukee, Wisconsin   Alex Molnar
November 1988   Barbara Lindquist

The Authors

Alex Molnar is professor of education at the University of Wisconsin, Milwaukee, and a family therapist. He received his B.A. degree (1966) in history from North Park College, his M.A. degree (1971) in history from Northeastern Illinois University, his Specialist's Certificate (1971) in educational administration from Southern Illinois University, Edwardsville, and his Ph.D. degree (1972) in urban education and M.S.W. degree (1980) from the University of Wisconsin, Milwaukee.

Molnar's principal scholarly interests are the relationship between social, political, and economic structure and school policies and procedures, and improving educational practice. He was editor of the 1985 Association for Supervision and Curriculum Development yearbook, *Current Thought on Curriculum,* and the 1987 volume, *Social Issues and Education: Challenge and Responsibility.* Molnar is consultant to *Educational Leadership* for its "Contemporary Issues" feature and the author of numerous articles on educational policy and practice.

Since 1984 Molnar has been a clinical member of the American Association for Marriage and Family Therapy. He has presented papers and published numerous articles on family therapy and on the educational applications of methods used by therapists to help families change. His work has been translated into Dutch, German, Spanish, and Japanese.

Molnar presents frequently at professional conferences and has consulted with school districts throughout the country.

Barbara Lindquist is a psychotherapist at the Washington County Mental Health Center in West Bend, Wisconsin. She is the coordinator of the Elder Peer Counseling Program, a joint project of the Washington County Mental Health Center and the Washington County Office on Aging. Lindquist trains and supervises older adult volunteers who provide paraprofessional counseling to their peers in the community. She received her B.S. degree (1979) in social work and her M.S.W. degree (1982) from the University of Wisconsin, Milwaukee. She completed a year of postgraduate training (1983) in the theory and practice of systemic family therapy at the Brief Family Therapy Center, Wisconsin Institute on Family Studies, Milwaukee, Wisconsin.

Lindquist is codeveloper of "Making Schools Work," a course for education professionals that teaches them how to apply ideas from ecosystemic family therapy to educational problems. She has authored several articles, has made presentations at national conferences in the fields of family therapy and education, and has made numerous in-service presentations to educators in the United States and West Germany. Lindquist has consistently been interested in the application of ecosystemic ideas to the treatment of diverse problems. These range from the psychological aspect of physical illness and disability, reflected in her article "Die Rolle der Familie in der Psychologie des Schmerzes" (The role of the family in the psychological aspect of chronic pain) (1984), to her work with educators and families on school-related problems, reflected in the article "Working with School Related Problems Without Going to School" (1987, with A. Molnar and L. Brauckmann), as well as many other articles in this area.

Changing Problem Behavior
in Schools

1

Why Is It So Difficult to Change Behavior?

An educator's life is filled with problems. This is not necessarily bad. Indeed, the satisfaction of solving problems such as Billy's failure to pay attention in reading group, Cathy's constant complaining about social studies homework, Sam's tardiness, or Kim's short temper is considered by many to be one of the rewards of an education career. Anyone who expects a problem-free career, or even a problem-free week, is doomed to perpetual frustration. Life is, as Dorothy L. Sayers's detective hero Lord Peter Wimsey is reportedly fond of saying, "one damn thing after another." No approach to addressing problems is likely to change this. However, it *is* possible for educators who find themselves doing the same unsuccessful thing over and over again to transform their perception of that situation and solve their problem.

Our approach to transforming problem situations is not based on the diagnosis of individuals with problems. Any teacher who has referred a child for psychological evaluation in the hope of learning how to solve a classroom problem knows that the diagnosis of the presumed cause of a behavior by no means necessarily provides any specific guidance about how to change it. When a diagnosis does not provide a practical guide for action, educators will tend to be guided by their "common sense." Sometimes actions based on these commonsense views change the problem situation satisfactorily. However, in our judgment, when these actions do not result in the desired change, the educator's

1

commonsense view (as well as the actions that flow from it) is part of the problem.

Whether you are a teacher, school psychologist, school counselor, school social worker, or school administrator, this book is intended to help you solve problems that have defied solution despite elaborate diagnoses or repeated applications of common sense. In this chapter we discuss where commonsense views come from and why they are so difficult to change.

Social Environments and Perception

In their book *The View from the Oak,* Kohl and Kohl (1977) use von Uexkull's concept of umwelt to explain how humans and animals organize their experience of the world. According to Kohl and Kohl, although many creatures share the same physical environment, they live in different worlds of experience. It is a creature's organization of experience (umwelt) that holds the key to understanding its behavior.

Since the nature of reality for a creature is a function of how that creature organizes experience, different patterns of organization will produce different perceptions and behaviors consistent with those perceptions. The umwelt of human beings is defined not only by the biological boundaries imposed by our senses but also by our social environment. It is our social environment that shapes the meanings we assign to those phenomena that we are biologically capable of sensing. We "construct" reality using the information provided by our senses and the meanings we assign to that information.

In *Small Futures* (1979), de Lone argues that certain general social factors, such as social class and race, constitute "master settings" that, operating through more intimate social groups such as our family, neighborhood, and school, shape our consciousness. Coles's *Children of Crisis* books (1967, 1971a, 1971b, 1977a, 1977b) tend to support this view. Coles found, for example, that there are important differences between what children from different social classes and ethnic groups perceive as possible accomplishments. Rubin (1976) maintains, in an analysis of the social environment of the working class in the United States, that characteristics that are usually described as manifestations of an individual's personality, such as passivity or resignation, can also be seen as simply the realistic responses of people to their social environment.

Together the work of de Lone, Coles, and Rubin paints a picture of human society in which multiple worlds of experience coexist. Since these worlds of experience are created and transformed by our participation in social systems, the meanings we assign to our behavior and the behavior of others are influenced by our past and present experiences in social settings. From this point of view, individuals will change their behavior in a given social system when changes in the interactions in that social system allow them to perceive different behaviors as appropriate and possible.

Perception and Behavior

Just as different species who share a common physical environment will experience that environment differently for biologically determined reasons, the work of de Lone, Coles, and Rubin suggests that human beings who share a common physical environment (a school building, for eample) may interpret the meaning of events within that environment very differently for reasons influenced by social factors.

According to Miller (1985), what we perceive is the result of sensation, attention, past experience, and expectation. Sensation is to a large measure determined by our biological capacities. However, our attention to, interpretation of, and expectation from what we sense are organized using an ideational framework we have constructed as a result of previous social interactions. In other words, perception is an active process in which we draw on our social history to assign meaning to what we are presently sensing.

It is the meaning we attribute to an event (Sam's tardiness, for example) that instructs us *how* to act (a stern reprimand or a wink and a smile) in response. If your nephew comes to your home for a visit, sits quietly, and has little to say, your reaction to him will, to a large extent, be determined by your ideas about the meaning of his behavior. If you regard his behavior as manipulative, you would react one way; if you consider his behavior as legitimate because he is "by nature" shy, you would react differently; and if you believed that he was silent because he wanted to listen attentively to everything you might say out of respect for your views, you would react still differently.

A further example should help emphasize the point. A teacher observes a student get up from her desk, walk to the pencil sharpener, and start to sharpen her pencil. There can be little dispute about what the student did. However, the teacher's response will not be based on the *fact* that the student got up from her desk, walked to the pencil sharpener, and started sharpening her pencil. The teacher's response will be based on the *meaning* that fact has for him or her. Was the student's behavior an act of defiance? An act of interest and involvement? An act of absentmindedness? Each of these possible interpretations would elicit different teacher responses.

Resolving Conflicting Perceptions

Obviously, life is not quite as simple as our examples have suggested. A person often has a number of ideas about what something means, and sometimes these ideas conflict. A student who repeatedly verbally taunts other students during a lesson may be demonstrating behavior that to the teacher may mean he or she:

- Has a learning disability
- Wants to "get" the teacher
- Comes from a "broken" home
- Needs extra attention
- Needs swift discipline
- Has poor social skills
- Is bored by the lesson
- Some or all of the above

It is common for one person to hold competing and apparently conflicting ideas about the meaning of another person's behavior. The question of how such ideational conflicts are resolved has been discussed by Festinger (1957) and Bateson (1972, 1979) in complementary analyses.

Festinger (1957) puts forward what he calls a theory of

cognitive dissonance. In general, Festinger postulates that when a person holds ideas that appear to conflict, that person will attempt to eliminate the cognitive dissonance this conflict creates by discarding one of the views or by adding new cognitive elements that support one view, reduce the importance of the dissonance, or bring the previously dissonant views into harmony. He argues that the pressure to eliminate cognitive dissonance is directly related to the importance of the views in conflict. Thus ideas that are both regarded as important and roughly equal in their attractiveness will produce the highest levels of dissonance and the strongest pressure to eliminate it.

The Influence of Prior Learning. Bateson (1972, 1979) suggests that in instances in which apparently contradictory ideas are held by a person, it is the most abstract or generalizable idea (the idea that has been used most successfully most often) that will survive. This suggests that if a teacher has frequently worked effectively with children who verbally taunt others during lessons by interpreting that behavior to mean that such children have poor social skills, the teacher is probably going to respond to this child's verbal taunting in a way consistent with the belief that the child has poor social skills, even if the teacher recognizes intellectually that there may be other good explanations for the behavior.

Because of the way the teacher in this example perceives the situation, if the problem behavior continues, the difficulty he or she faces is how to reconcile two dissonant propositions:

Proposition 1:   Students verbally taunt other students during lessons because they lack social skills.
Proposition 2:   This student did not stop his or her verbal taunting when taught social skills, so there must be some other explanation for the taunting.

The student is behaving in a way (taunting verbally) that, to the teacher, means he or she lacks social skills, and yet this student's taunting behavior continued after he or she was taught social skills.

Using Bateson's thoughts about the preeminence of more abstract ideas (those used most successfully most often) over less abstract ideas, we would predict that the teacher will disregard proposition 2. Thus the very success of the "lack of social skills" explanation in helping the teacher stop instances of verbal taunting behavior in previous situations becomes an obstacle to him or her in formulating or accepting a new idea about why this particular student is not responding in the way he or she "is supposed to." We might also predict that the teacher will be puzzled by the student's apparent "resistance" to "effective" strategies and will seek ways to "overcome" this "resistance" that are compatible with the idea that the student is acting this way because he or she lacks social skills or is deficient in some unusual way.

The Influence of Social-Group Support. Festinger's ideas can also help us understand another reason why the teacher in our example might disregard proposition 2. Festinger maintains that the social support present for one of the cognitive elements in a dissonant relationship is one of the most powerful determinants of which cognitive elements will be retained. In his discussion of mass phenomena, Festinger cites instances in which social support within groups for beliefs that were demonstrably false, actually strengthened those beliefs, in spite of their obvious falsehood. For example, he describes a nineteenth-century religious group that predicted the world would end on a particular date. After the predicted date of the earth's destruction had come and gone, the group found a way of explaining why their first prediction was incorrect and selected a new date for earth's destruction. Their belief in the prophecy that the world would end actually intensified as a result. The social support educators receive from their professional peers for explanations of problem behavior that fail to lead to acceptable results may, in a similar way, help to strengthen those explanations, even in the face of repeated failure.

Institutions also help codify the support of professional peers. Schools have long institutional memories. Each year a child is in school, the meaning of her or his behavior becomes more embedded in the school's official records and in the informal network that passes information about the meaning of that child's behavior from one school official to the next. In a sense, as children move through school, their behavior is increasingly understood by making reference to the "frozen" perceptions of their past behavior. Institutional records, formal and informal, can be powerful devices for maintaining the behavior of educators and students in problem patterns because they contribute to maintaining unhelpful interpretations of that behavior.

In addition to their professional peers, educators have other powerful sources of social support for the meanings they assign to behavior. In a description of factors that shape a child's perception of social reality (equally applicable to adults), de Lone (1979) writes, "We are suggesting that the experiences characteristic of different social class and racial situations, plus the history of the group to which an individual belongs, come together to realize their developmental impact in the child's theory of social reality" (p. 161). de Lone suggests that these environmental messages function both consciously and unconsciously. In other words, the teacher in our example as well as the child that teacher hopes to educate carry inside themselves racial, cultural, and gender-related experiential histories that shape and support the meanings they assign to the behavior in question. It is not surprising that the same behavior may have very different meanings, for example, for a middle-class teacher and a working-class student. It is also not surprising that a person whose interpretation of events is shared by a large number of other people whom that person regards as significant is not likely to readily change his or her interpretation, even when faced with a chronic problem.

If we accept Bateson's and Festinger's views, we can see that there are good reasons why the teacher in our example might continue to believe and act as if the taunting behavior of the student is a consequence of poor social skills, even if attempts to change this student's behavior based on this interpretation repeatedly fail to produce the desired results.

The Influence of Cause-Effect Reasoning. We have explained the stability of individual perceptions in problematic situations in terms of prior learning and in terms of social support. There is an additional factor. In Western culture, although the meanings an individual assigns to behavior may be derived from prior experiences in social settings, the general framework used to relate to various meanings associated with a given behavior is cause-effect reasoning. In the West, the belief that reality can best be understood in terms of cause-effect relationships is so much assumed as to be rarely accessible to analysis or challenge. For example, when a child acts in a way his or her teacher finds objectionable, the teacher will, in considering how to change the student's behavior, use the belief in cause and effect in the form of a mental rule. This mental rule can be outlined as a series of assumptions:

1. All behavior has a cause, and therefore all behavior is an effect of something else.
2. Cause precedes and therefore controls effect.
3. To remove the effect, the cause must be removed.

Examples that can be used to illustrate the "truth" that reality can best be explained by cause-effect relationships are too numerous to catalogue. People looking for proof of the validity of cause-effect reasoning might point out, for example, that when the alarm clock sounds (cause), they wake up (effect). However, in problem situations the issue is less the "truth" of a cause-effect explanation of problem behavior than the usefulness of that explanation as a basis for changing the behavior.

In many instances, cause-effect logic helps to achieve the desired results. For example, a teacher who believes that the cause of Lyle's giggling is his proximity to Patrice might change where Lyle sits and effectively solve the problem. In this example, the teacher's belief that Lyle's giggling was caused by his proximity to Patrice led to an effective action to solve the problem: changing where Lyle sat. However, suppose that the teacher believed that the cause of Lyle's behavior was that he came from a single-parent family? In this instance, the remedy that might logically flow from that interpretation is not clear at all.

The assumption that for every effect there is *a* cause helps to keep problem-solving efforts focused on problem individuals. Furthermore, once it is assumed that the behavior of a given individual is the problem, then that person's behavior can be diagnosed to help find *its* cause. The logic is that if the cause can be identified, a "treatment" can be devised to eliminate the "symptom" (that is, to change the behavior of the problem person). The process of reducing behavior to ever smaller elements in an attempt to find its cause makes it difficult to see behavior in its context and to consider the full variety of explanations that might be helpful in changing things for the better.

Change is difficult in chronic problem situations, because the points of view and the behaviors of the people involved, sustained by prior learning, social support, and cause-effect reasoning, become liabilities. Each of these factors functions to maintain the problem by locking in people's perceptions. Chronic problem situations are characterized by stability. Solutions require change in the behaviors or the perceptions of the people involved or in both. No one can change past experiences. However, the past need not control behavior in the present. *Changing Problem Behavior in Schools* is devoted to helping you learn how to make changes in problem situations you face right now and to encouraging you to do so.

2

When You Want
Something to Change,
You Must Change Something

The framework we use to relate the various factors that influence people's perceptions and behavior is the concept of ecosystem. The concept of ecosystem allows us to focus on the relatedness of behavior in a social setting such as a classroom or school and provides us with a way of explaining individual behavior that does not require cause-effect logic.

The view of relatedness and change among people and between people and their environment that we call ecosystemic has been discussed in a number of fields, including natural science and astronomy (Lovelock and Margulis, 1986), sport psychology (Grau, Müller, and Gunnarsson, 1987), agriculture (Rodale, 1983), family therapy (de Shazer, 1982; Bogdan, 1984, 1986, 1987), community development (Bercuvitz, 1987), and science fiction (Asimov, 1982). Even the theory of evolution does not require a cause-effect explanation for change (Gould, 1977, 1982). Accident and sudden catastrophe can be used more effectively to explain evolutionary change than the gradual impact of countless small "causes."

The complex and varied relationships that constitute an ecosystem need not be seen as causing each other. A description of the natural world that suggests that sheep cause wolves because wolves prey on sheep, flowers cause bees because bees use the nectar from flowers, or salmon cause bears because bears eat salmon is not sustainable. However, it seems sound to point out that the behavior of wolves is influenced by the presence of sheep, the behavior of bees is influenced by the presence of flowers, and the behavior of bears

10

is influenced by the presence of salmon, and vice versa. If modern civilization has made one thing abundantly clear, it is that when something, even something quite small, in an ecosystem changes, related changes manifest themselves throughout that ecosystem.

In ecosystemic terms, a teacher and his or her students are part of a classroom ecosystem and are therefore influenced by the ecosystemic relations in that classroom. A teacher's perceptions and classroom behavior are part of a pattern of perceptions and behaviors that influences and is influenced by (but does not cause) the perceptions and behaviors of everyone else in the classroom, and vice versa.

There are numerous examples of functioning ecosystems in both our private and our professional lives. Consider the seating arrangement at the family dinner table. If you live in a family in which there is a common family mealtime and each person usually sits in the same place, your family will behave differently if one person sits in the "wrong" place. The person whose place has been taken must decide what to do. Even if he or she simply sits in a different chair, another family member will be displaced and the usual seating pattern changed. The person whose usual place at the table has been taken as well as every other family member will interpret what has happened and will act accordingly.

In another instance, a family member might have had a difficult day at work or school and come home acting very differently than usual. An otherwise friendly, cooperative spouse or child may suddenly seem to be a disgruntled crank who is impossible to please. That person's mood and actions initiate patterns of interaction that influence everyone in the family to varying degrees.

In a complex ecosystem such as a family, a change in one person's behavior influences the ecosystem in a number of ways with varying strengths. In some families, taking someone else's seat at the dinner table or coming home crabby might lead to a fistfight; in others, it might be an occasion for humor. Although it is not possible to predict precisely what the changes in the situation will be, it is possible to predict that *when something in an ecosystem changes, the ecosystem will change.*

In a classroom, the relatedness of behaviors can be seen when, for example, one student blurts out something silly during a lesson, and, as if in a chain reaction, other students laugh and begin to misbehave; or a teacher does not respond to student questions, and the students begin to be sarcastic to one another; or a student who is not normally moody comes to class obviously sad, and students who might otherwise tease him or her go out of their way to be nice. In school, if a colleague who is ordinarily friendly and easily approached walks by you one morning in the hall without greeting you or acknowledging your presence, this behavior change will most likely affect your behavior. You might pursue your colleague to determine if something is wrong; you might withdraw, worrying that you have somehow offended him or her; or you might involve others by asking if they noticed the change, too. However you respond, you will have been influenced by the change in your colleague's behavior. In an ecosystem, it cannot be otherwise.

An Ecology of Ideas

The social world of the school (teachers and students together in a classroom, or colleagues together in a staff meeting, for example) represents what Bateson (1972, 1979) considered an ecology of ideas. Simply put, individuals have ideas about the behavior of other group members, they have ideas about group actions, they have ideas about the ideas of others, they have ideas about the ideas of others' ideas of them, and so on. The interaction of these ideas via behavior constitutes the ecology of ideas that *is* the experienced social context (classroom, family, bowling team, for example) of individuals. By describing a school or classroom as an ecology of ideas, we can make a clear distinction between its physical artifacts—such as the room in which a class meets, the desks at which students sit, and the textbooks used—and the meanings those artifacts and the behaviors that occur in that space have for the individuals who occupy it.

Although a social group is defined by the predictable interaction patterns that occur among group members, these patterns are not necessarily dependent on group members sharing a common idea about the meaning of individual behaviors. Predictable patterns of interaction can occur without a common idea about the meaning of a given behavior. It is necessary, however, that each individual regard his or her behavior and the behavior of the others in the group as generally consistent with the meaning he or she has assigned to those behaviors. In this manner, although group members may assign divergent meanings to individual behaviors, each member has the meaning he or she assigns to that behavior affirmed. Thus, in any group, a single behavior may be consistent with and therefore supportive of a variety of divergent meanings. For example, a teacher (Fred) may believe that a particular student is a bully, the student (Alice) may regard herself as a beleaguered outsider who must be ever vigilant to protect her rights, and a fellow student (Joe) may view her as admirably independent of adult authority. When Alice gets into a shoving match with Darien over an incident in the hallway, Fred will see confirmation that Alice is a bully; Alice will believe even more strongly that it is necessary to guard her rights. When Fred behaves toward Alice as if she were a bully, this will further strengthen Alice's belief that she must protect her rights (because it will be obvious to her that the teacher will not). If Alice reacts aggressively in response to Fred's attempt to discipline her, Joe will see confirmation that Alice is admirably independent. Although the people in this example have very different ideas about the meanings of their own behavior and that of the others, each person had his or her view confirmed and strengthened by the events described.

For the most part, the fact that individuals assign widely divergent meanings to the same behavior is of little practical interest, because the patterns of group interaction that support these interpretations are not considered problematic. However, considering the meanings assigned to behavior deemed problematic is important, because in problem situations these assigned meanings are part of the problem.

Initiating Change

If we think of classrooms and schools as ecosystems consisting of the interacting ideas and behaviors of students and educators, it is not necessary to find *a* cause for problem behavior. It is enough to know that a change in the ideas or the behaviors of any person in the classroom or school will influence the behaviors and ideas of every person in the classroom and school.

Not all stable patterns of interaction in a classroom or school represent problems. However, since all chronic problem behaviors are part of a stable pattern of thought and action, the functional definition of a solution is a change in the problematic pattern that is in some way considered desirable. When an educator finds himself or herself repeatedly doing the same thing in response to a problem behavior without satisfactory results, that pattern is at once a stable characteristic of the ecosystem and a reason to change.

From an ecosystemic perspective, initiating change in a chronic problem situation involves two possible practical activities: (1) identifying new interpretations of the behavior considered to be a problem that fit the facts at hand and behaving in ways consistent with these new interpretations or (2) simply behaving differently. It is difficult to proceed this way using a cause-effect perspective, because considering new interpretations requires rejecting or at least challenging an interpretation (or cause) that had previously been regarded as the truth. Furthermore, it follows from cause-effect logic that if a previously held interpretation is rejected, it should be replaced with a new interpretation that is then to be regarded as the true explanation (or cause) of the behavior in question. Since ecosystemic logic holds that in a social environment all ideas and behavior interact with and influence each other in continuous patterns of interaction, the attributed "cause" of a behavior can never be established as the truth. Ecosystemically, the truth is a function of the point at which an observer begins and ends ("punctuates") the observation of a pattern of interactions. If one punctuation does not help to change things, others can be used without fear of abandoning the truth.

Punctuating Behavior

Schools and classrooms are full of examples of how different punctuations produce different attributions of causality for the same problematic behaviors. The following seven events have been arranged in different sequences to demonstrate how the same events can be punctuated in many different ways.

Punctuation A

Student 1 teases student 2's sister on the way to school.
Student 2 hits student 1 at recess.
Student 1 pushes student 2 in lunch line.
Teacher punishes student 1.
Student 1 teases student 2 in class.
Student 2 threatens student 1 in class.
Teacher punishes student 2.

Punctuation B

Student 1 pushes student 2 in lunch line.
Teacher punishes student 1.
Student 1 teases student 2 in class.
Student 2 threatens student 1 in class.
Teacher punishes student 2.
Student 1 teases student 2's sister on the way to school.
Student 2 hits student 1 at recess.

Punctuation C

Student 2 threatens student 1 in class.
Teacher punishes student 2.
Student 1 teases student 2's sister on the way to school.
Student 2 hits student 1 at recess.
Student 1 pushes student 2 in lunch line.
Teacher punishes student 1.
Student 1 teases student 2 in class.

To illustrate our point, we have manipulated the temporal order of events in the preceding sequence in a way that is not possible in real life. When only the seven events in our example are considered, something happened first, second, and so on. In real life, it is the selection of events used to explain something that constitutes the punctuation that attributes causality. Change the events included, and you modify the attribution of causality, because different events are then seen as happening first, second, third, and so on. From an ecosystemic perspective, the various ways of punctuating a series of events cannot be distinguished by the truth of one view and the falsity of the others. Each view is, given its perspective, "true." Thus, in considering problem behavior, the application of ecosystemic logic calls not for the identification of the "true" cause of the problem but rather for the identification of an interpretation that fits the facts at hand and suggests new behaviors that might change the situation in an acceptable way.

Problems and Solutions

Thinking about schools and classrooms as ecosystems is a hopeful way of approaching problems, because it tells you that you can influence problem behaviors by what you do in school. As a part of the ecosystem of the classroom or school, your thoughts, attitudes, and behavior influence the thoughts, attitudes, and behavior of the people with whom you share the classroom and school. In other words, you can influence problem behavior by changing yourself.

Our first case example illustrates how, by applying his knowledge of ecosystemic functioning, a teacher who was feeling harassed by a colleague changed his behavior and was able to solve his problem without ever confronting it directly.

Case examples in books sometimes seem too good to be true. However, although we have changed the names and other identifying characteristics, the following case example and all the other case examples in *Changing Problem Behavior in Schools* are based on actual situations described by students who have taken our "Making Schools Work" course over the last six years.

Case Example: Unwanted Attention

My wife and I are in a somewhat unique situation in that she and I are teaching together in the same school building this year. This has not proven to be a problem; in fact, it has its good points. However, there is a fellow teacher, Cynthia, who made comments concerning our relationship. Most of these comments were petty, and I should not have let them bother me in the least. But, unfortunately, they did tend to bother me. For example, several weeks ago my wife and I both ate hot lunches on trays in the lounge. When we were done, I asked Constance, my wife, if she would mind taking my tray back, as she had to walk past the lunchroom anyway.

Cynthia then chirped in with, "Boy, Constance, I sure would like to know what the hold is Larry has over you." As usual, this remark was made in a loud voice in the presence of many co-workers. Granted, it was petty, but I was tired of hearing comments like this made day after day after day. Anytime she could get a comment in about our relationship, our roles at home, and so on, she did. I seethed inside while appearing to stay calm and ignored the comments, because I did not think that they deserved a reply.

After learning ecosystemic techniques, I was ready to try one of two suggested methods. For example, I thought of saying, "Cynthia, I really do appreciate your genuine interest in our relationship." However, I truly felt uncomfortable with that approach. I felt that I would come across as being a bit sarcastic. So instead I decided not to focus on the point of the problem. After all, if you change any part of an ecosystem, the ecosystem is changed. With this in mind, I set out to change things. I began first by being as friendly to Cynthia as I sincerely could. When I ran into her, I greeted her with a "good morning" or "good day." Then I began casually to draw her into short conversations—initially by seeking her advice regarding a mutual student. Then I shared some information I obtained from a parent-teacher conference regarding another student. In the past, I had shied away from this woman because of her comments. This was a complete turnaround for me. I continued to be friendly and nice and to engage her in conversation when I could. Well . . . Cynthia has begun to greet me when we meet. She has stopped making annoying comments about my relationship with my wife. In all honesty, I do not know if it is because of my "changing the ecosystem." I do know that, as of now, I am pleased.

In an ecosystem, problem behavior is only one part of any pattern of behavioral interactions. Therefore, a problem is defined as the behavior identified as the problem behavior and the responses to that behavior. For example, if a child repeatedly speaks out of turn and his or her teacher repeatedly responds by explaining that the child should wait to be called on, the teacher's response is part of the problem. If every time a child does not hand in his or her homework, he or she is made to stay in at recess but continues not to hand in homework, the problem is both the student not handing in homework and the teacher having him or her stay in at recess. If the responses to a problem behavior are not changing the problem situation, they are helping to maintain it.

In order for a problem to be considered solved, one or both of the following must happen: (1) The behavior considered problematic is changed in an acceptable way; (2) the interpretation of the problem behavior changes so that the behavior is no longer considered a problem. Number one is self-explanatory. If a person stops doing something that you consider to be a problem, the problem is solved. Number two requires some explaining. Consider the example of the problem a kindergarten teacher was having with one of her students. When the class had free time and could choose from among several activities in the classroom, if the student did not get her first choice of activity, she would, in the teacher's words, "pout" and act like a "spoiled brat." When asked to describe the student's behavior, the teacher reported that the student would stand near the activity that was her first choice and watch without comment or sometimes cry as the other students began doing the activity she wanted to do. This behavior would continue for up to ten minutes before the student would move on to her second activity choice.

By chance, the kindergarten teacher learned that at the school the child had previously attended, the behavior modification technique of "time-out" had been used. With this information, the teacher reinterpreted the student's behavior. The teacher decided that rather than pouting, this student was "timing herself out." It was no longer a problem for the teacher when the student stood by her first-choice activity for a while and "timed herself out" before going on to another activity. In other words, behavior that was a problem for the teacher when it was interpreted as "pouting" and acting "spoiled" was solved when the teacher interpreted it as taking a "time-out."

Sometimes a solution includes a change in both the problematic behavior and the interpretation of the behavior, as the conclusion of this kindergarten example shows. Once the teacher had interpreted the student's behavior as "timing herself out," she commented to the student on how creative she was at being able to use what she had learned at her other school to help her in this new school. She complimented the student on her ability to transfer the skill from one situation to another. For the teacher, the problem behavior was no longer a problem because of the new meaning it held for her, so the student's behavior could have continued. However, when the teacher quite understandably acted on the new interpretation of the student's behavior and changed her own behavior by complimenting the student, the student's behavior also changed, and her "time-outs" went from ten minutes to two or three minutes in length.

Any alternative explanation that helps you to behave differently in relation to the behavior you consider problematic has the potential to lead to a solution. However, not every alternative explanation is equally good at suggesting behavioral change. Explanations for a child's problem behavior based on past events ("she comes from a broken home," "he is a middle child," "she was abused three years earlier," "he was held back in second grade," and so on) often offer little or no help in figuring out how or why you should change your own behavior. No one can change the past. Explanations based on the present situation in which the problem occurs will better illuminate possibilities for change in your behavior.

If your customary response to a child who is frequently tardy to your class is to threaten and to carry out a variety of punishments, and the child's response is to continue to be tardy and to meet each of your threats and punishments with his or her own escalating defiance, then changing something *in the situation* is called for. Sometimes explanations based on past events may help you to change your behavior in a problem situation. However, often people in chronic problem situations seem to use this type of explanation to justify rather than to change the problematic state of affairs.

Past-oriented explanations of problem behavior tend to catalogue misery, inadequacy, and invariability. The problem person is seen as the victim of some life circumstance (such as being born the middle child) or afflicted with some quasi-medical-sounding disorder (such as having a learning disability). In almost every instance, the description is not positive, and the focus of change is invariably on the problem person. Indeed, explanations for problem behavior are often no more than none-too-flattering characterizations of the person whose behavior is considered problematic. Consider two different ways of explaining the following "problem" behavior: nonattendance of parents at school open house or parent-teacher conferences. These parents can be described as disinterested in the schooling of their children and generally uninvolved in school activities. However, another way of viewing these parents might be that they are parents who trust educators and have confidence in the teachers' knowledge and ability to instruct their children. This is, after all, a task for which educators have been specially trained, and the parents have not. This might be the parents' way of trying to cooperate with the school by not interfering. No doubt you have a preference for one of these explanations; so do we. From an ecosystemic perspective, the point is not that one of them is true and the other false. The point is that if the explanation selected by the educator who is experiencing a problem is not working to produce change, another explanation should be tried.

Adopting a Cooperative Perspective

At first glance, the difficulty of what we are proposing may seem overwhelming. After all, people *believe* their explanations. Indeed, as we discussed in Chapter One, the inability of a person's explanation to produce constructive change in a problem situation does not necessarily mean that person will change his or her view. Taylor and Brown (1988), in their discussion of social judgment, point out that people are not disinterested assessors of information—quite the contrary. In the normal course of events, people try to make the data available to them come out in a way that best suits their particular theory. Fortunately, an ecosystemic approach allows people to adopt new explanations about behavior without rejecting old ones. Instead of rejecting your current interpretation of the problem behavior, you are asked to entertain the possibility that other explanations can also be true and that some of them may help you solve your problem. Sometimes it is easier to move in this direction by putting yourself in the other person's shoes and trying to see the problem situation as that person might. In general, seeing the problem as others in the situation might see it can help you see the rational and understandable reasons for behavior you had previously considered irrational and negative.

The ability to regard a person's problem behavior as understandable, given that person's perception of the situation, is the essence of what we call a cooperative perspective in problem solving. A cooperative perspective follows logically from the ecosystemic view that all behavior has multiple meanings and functions. If a teacher believes a student is capable of doing the required work but does not perform because she or he is lazy, the teacher will act in a way that, from that point of view, makes sense when dealing with a lazy, underachieving student. In whatever way the teacher decides to act, whether by reprimanding the student, referring the student for counseling or psychological evaluation, or involving the principal, the teacher's actions will be based on his or her perception of the situation, and, given the teacher's point of view, they will be quite understandable.

The student's perception of the circumstances might be that the work is too hard, that it is not relevant, or that it is repetitious and boring. In whatever way the student may perceive the situation, her or his behavior will be quite understandable given that perception. Therefore, in solving problems, it is helpful to accept that each person is behaving in a way that is understandable given her or his perception of the situation.

The teacher in the following case example describes how things changed when he tried to understand a student's "off-task" behavior from the student's perspective and responded accordingly.

Case Example: Two New Perspectives

Noel's off-task talking behavior was distracting for me, but I wanted to attempt to see what this socializing was doing for him.

After spending some time thinking about how the situation might look to Noel, I talked to him. I told him that I could see how important it was for him to talk to his friends during the day, and that he needed this time. Having close contact with other students was probably part of his learning style, and he probably learned from his friends. I stated that sometimes I knew he was quiet, while at other times he was noisier, and that everyone needs noisy as well as quiet times. I told Noel I thought he was cooperating in his own way during my teaching time with other groups, because he did not directly interrupt, and he stayed close to his desk when talking. I also said that talking did not stop him from doing most of his papers accurately, and that I recognized that he gives up other activities to talk. Finally, I let Noel know that I would try to understand he needed to talk during working times.

Noel seemed somewhat surprised. My changed perspective gave approval to his talking. His smile indicated to me that he was pleased that I knew how important his social contacts were. I was particularly struck by Noel's verbal response, "Sometimes I know I should be quiet and just work, so I will." At the time I was not sure if his comment was apologetic or defensive, but now I think he was showing understanding of my perspective, just as I had shown understanding of his.

Sometimes I think I have changed my perspective so well that I do not notice Noel's off-task talking behaviors. At other times I know that Noel has changed a little in response to the change I initiated in our classroom ecosystem.

I think my talk with Noel about understanding his need to socialize made such an impression that it made him exert more effort. The satisfaction we both feel and our cooperation must be evident to everyone in the class.

The first paragraph of the next case example illustrates how descriptions of a child's history and circumstances may be accurate but unhelpful in finding a solution for a problem in school. Once the teacher in this case example discovered how to cooperate with his student in the situation at hand, he also discovered a solution for his problem.

Case Example: The Runner

Billy is a first-grade repeater who came from a broken home. He has a history of being a very aggressive child. He had very few social skills and used to go out of his way to try and hurt other children, whether in physical education class, recess, or during the noon hour. Although he said that other children were at fault because they did something to him first, I had yet to witness this. His father has complicated matters by telling Billy that he had the right to defend himself against anyone who tried to harm him. Billy used this as his excuse. Whenever he hit someone, he said, "They started it, and my father told me I had the right to defend myself."

Billy had been a real trial not only in my class but also throughout the school. His father had been called to the school four times in the last month. Billy could be a real Jekyll and Hyde. One minute he would be fine, playing along with the rest of the children, and the next he would run up and purposefully slam into the back of a child, hit and kick him or her, and so on.

One day about three weeks ago, Billy came in and was running around gym class and not getting in his exercise position. This seemed like an ideal time to try cooperating with Billy. I told him, "I can see that you really have a lot of energy that needs to be used up before you will be ready for class. I want you to go to the other side of the gym and run for five minutes. I do not want you to come back into the class until you have done your five minutes of running. I will let you know when five minutes are up, and then you can join the rest of the class." This had an unexpected result. About half the class also wanted to run! I decided to let those who wanted to run with Billy. At first Billy objected, but I told him that these children had so much energy that they too had to run. He accepted my explanation. Most of the other children quit after one or two minutes, but Billy and one other boy continued to run for the full five minutes. After Billy had finished, I told him that from now on before every class he was to run for five minutes before joining the class. The gym is divided in two by a door, so I could watch the runners and conduct my class at the same time.

When Billy's next class time came, he went out of his way to remind me that I had promised to let him run for five minutes before joining the rest of the class. I expressed surprise that he remembered and also stated that I did not think he could run that long again. Billy joined the class after he completed his running, and for the first time in months, he did not touch or bother

anybody. I was amazed. The change in his behavior was unbeliev-
able, especially in light of his behavior throughout the year.

Cooperation offers a positive alternative to resistance as a
way of thinking about why a problem person does not change his
or her behavior. Most people in education are familiar with the
concept of resistance. This concept provides a negative explanation
for problem behavior that does not change. A person whose
behavior does not change in the face of repeated attempts at
problem solving is usually characterized as resistant and as having
bad motives for what he or she is doing. In contrast to resistance,
the concept of cooperation encourages people to consider the
problem situation from perspectives other than their own and to
look at the positive meanings and functions of a problem behavior.
For example, it is not uncommon for teachers to describe students
who repeatedly fail to do their homework as "resisting" learning or
for school psychologists to describe teachers who do not follow
through in the classroom with suggestions the psychologists have
made as "resisting" their efforts to help make things better.

These situations can be described differently using a cooperative perspective. The student's not doing homework can be
characterized as communicating to the teacher that the work is too
hard or too easy. Or, looking at the larger ecosystem of the
classroom, the student's not doing homework can be characterized
as a sacrifice she or he is making that helps to demonstrate to
classmates the problems not doing homework creates for students.
Either of these characterizations can help lead to new teacher
behaviors and possibly a solution to the problem.

Instead of resisting efforts to make things better, the teacher
who does not adopt the school psychologist's suggestions (when
viewed from a cooperative perspective) might be described as being
motivated to proceed cautiously because he or she believes that
rushing ahead might make matters worse for the student. This
perspective is much more likely to enable the psychologist to
establish a positive relationship with the teacher than a perspective
that characterizes the teacher as someone whose resistance must be
overcome.

Since the concept of cooperation encourages the use of

positive explanations of the behavior of others, it also helps to avoid struggles and to construct solutions in which there are only winners instead of winners and losers.

The children's book *Bread and Jam for Frances,* by Russell Hoban (1964), depicts a situation in which adults and children frequently find themselves, one in which an adult wants a child to do one thing and the child wants to do something different. The question is, how shall the adults and the child cooperate to find a solution without creating losers? The problem in *Bread and Jam for Frances* is that Frances's parents want her to try various kinds of foods, and Frances wants to eat only bread and jam. Frances's parents make several attempts to entice her to eat eggs or cereal for breakfast or salami sandwiches for lunch or spaghetti or pork chops for dinner, all the while pointing out the merits of such variety. Frances steadfastly holds to the advantages of knowing exactly the taste and texture of what she is going to eat.

Frances's parents decide to cooperate with her and accept her point of view. They begin serving her bread and jam for breakfast, lunch, after-school snacks, dinner, and bedtime snacks. After two days of bread and jam, Frances begins to ask her parents whether they are not afraid her teeth might rot and why she is not served the same food for dinner as everyone else. When her parents respond by saying they thought she liked only bread and jam, Frances cries and asks how will they know what she likes if they do not allow her to try other foods. Frances' parents then oblige her by giving her a variety of foods, which she eats with pleasure.

It may seem a big leap from Frances to a high school gang member. However, just as Frances and her parents found a way to solve their problem without anyone being defeated, the teacher in our final example learned to cooperate with his student in a situation that, at first glance, did not seem promising.

Case Example: A Valuable Resource

Leo used to write gang symbols on his hands, arms, books, and papers that he turned in. I had tried to stop him. I had called his parents, sent him to the vice-principal, caused him to be suspended, refused to accept work submitted with gang symbols on it, and had him wash off symbols in class.

I feared that the next step after writing gang symbols would be Leo's joining a gang and becoming involved with gang activities. I wanted to change him. However, despite my best efforts, Leo never really changed, so I decided that I would.

The next time I saw Leo with gang symbols on his hand, I got a piece of paper and copied the symbol. Leo asked me what I was doing, and I replied that I was going to be teaching in that school for many more years and had decided to learn as much about the gangs as I could. I told Leo that I realized that people join gangs mainly for fear or for social reasons.

When Leo turned in his notebook at the end of the week, I copied the gang symbols off the covers and tore out a couple of pages, but only, as I told Leo, "to photocopy them."

Lately I have seen no gang symbols coming from Leo other than a few signs passed to friends using hand symbols. The work that Leo turns in is also free of symbols.

Clearly, this teacher's ability to cooperate with Leo has paid dividends. Instead of symbols of defiance, Leo's gang symbols became a useful resource to his teacher. Whether Leo stopped writing the symbols or not, by cooperating instead of struggling, this teacher found a starting point for positively changing his relationship with Leo.

A Hopeful Possibility

Many of the ideas we describe as ecosystemic have been discussed in the psychotherapy literature for over two decades, usually under the rubric of systemic, strategic, or structural approaches to therapy (Bertalanffy, 1966; Haley, 1973, 1978; Minuchin, 1974; Watzlawick, Weakland, and Fisch, 1974; Whitaker, 1975; Aponte, 1976; Bernard and Corrales, 1979; Frykman, 1984; de Shazer, 1982, 1985). Although not yet widely discussed in educational literature, the utility of these ideas for school psychologists (Howard, 1980; Maher, 1981; Anderson, 1983; Bowman and Goldberg, 1983; Hannafin and Witt, 1983; Wendt and Zake, 1984; Kral, 1986), school counselors (Amatea and Fabrick, 1981; Worden, 1981; Golden, 1983), school social workers (Huslage and Stein, 1985), special education teachers (Mandel and others, 1975; Fish and Shashi, 1985), and school administrators (Molnar, 1986) has been explored. The value of systemic, strategic, and structural ideas in helping solve school and classroom problems and problems between schools and families is a subject of increasing professional interest (Tucker and Dyson, 1976; Smith, 1978; Johnston and Fields, 1981; McDaniel, 1981; Fine and Holt, 1983; Pfeiffer and Tittler, 1983; Berger, 1984; Foster, 1984; Hansen, 1984; Okun, 1984; Williams and Weeks, 1984; Ergenziner, 1985; Power and Bartholomew, 1985; DiCocco, 1986; Lindquist, Molnar, and Brauckmann, 1987).

Molnar and Lindquist have described a variety of ways in which teachers and other school professionals can use ecosystemic concepts and techniques to solve classroom and school problems (Molnar and Lindquist, 1982, 1984a, 1984b, 1985, 1988; Molnar, Lindquist, and Hage, 1985). As a result of having developed and taught the course "Making Schools Work," we have gathered over two hundred case studies that demonstrate how ecosystemic ideas have been used by teachers and other education professionals in schools and classrooms. These case studies document successes in a variety of settings and situations (classrooms, teachers' lounges, parent conferences) to solve a variety of problems such as those involving (1) students (tardiness, sleeping in class, refusal to do homework, talking out in class, fighting), (2) staff relations (lack of participation in instructional improvement programs, lack of cooperation in curriculum implementation, interpersonal conflicts, disagreement over the placement of children in special programs), and (3) the school and community (lack of cooperation between school personnel and parents, poor communication between the school and parents).

Quite apart from what the literature may or may not say or what the experience of other people who have tried ecosystemic ideas has been, there are a number of reasons why you may find them appealing. Ecosystemic ideas are "user friendly." Thinking about a chronic problem ecosystemically does not mean you must abandon your accustomed methods of solving problems. Ecosystemic methods offer a framework for thinking differently about a problem that has gotten the better of you, so you have an alternative to doing the same thing "harder" and "louder" when it obviously is not helping. Although learning to view student behavior ecosystemically most often requires abandoning "commonsense" explanations and solutions, it also makes things easier for you. It makes it easier for you to view the behavior of each person in the classroom and school as part of any problem and as a possible contributor to a solution; to focus on change in the problem situation; and to consider divergent explanations for problem behavior. Perhaps most important of all, it encourages you to consider what the problem person is doing that is functional and positive.

Although approaching problems ecosystemically may at first seem exotic, the ideas can be mastered without any specialized background knowledge. Since the focus is on change, not on diagnosis, ecosystemic techniques, guided by your professional judgment, can be used in a variety of problem situations (when students are sleeping in class, fighting, or not doing homework, for example). You do not have to adopt an elaborate system for managing behavior or a new and technical language for describing your problems in order to use these ideas. When you find yourself "stuck" in a problem situation, select the ecosystemic idea or technique that you are most comfortable with and that you believe is most appropriate to the situation and try it out.

3

Finding Solutions
in New Places

In Chapter One, we identified a number of reasons why you might find it difficult to change in problem situations even if you are not accomplishing your purposes. In Chapter Two, we described how problems and solutions are viewed from an ecosystemic perspective. In this chapter, we discuss your role in problem situations and how best to approach and understand the ecosystemic techniques detailed in Part Two.

As you may have guessed from our reference to detective hero Lord Peter Wimsey, we are English murder mystery fans. As any reader of English murder mysteries knows, in most stories there are a number of false starts in solving the crime, as the hero follows the various paths suggested by preliminary theories that seem to fit the facts but lead into blind alleys. However, in the end, the hero usually hits on a theory that allows the mystery to be solved. In putting the concepts described in the preceding chapters into practice in your school or classroom, it will be helpful to adopt an approach similar to that of an English murder mystery detective hero. We call this a "sleuthing" approach to problem situations.

In some ways detective heros have it easier than educators. When someone has been murdered, it can usually be said with assurance that someone else committed the murder. All the hero has to do is gather and organize the relevant facts into a theory that leads to the solution of the case. For educators, the "crime" is rarely so obvious as in detective fiction. Indeed, the very nature of the crime is often in dispute. Despite these difficulties, we can say with some confidence that when a problem becomes a chronic problem, it is a clue that your theory has led you into a blind alley, and that a new theory that also fits the facts is necessary. No detective gets to be a hero of detective fiction by insisting that his or her theory is correct even when it does not lead to a solution. Just so, educators are not likely to extract themselves from blind alleys by clinging to theories that have led them astray. A detective who continues to argue for the utility of his or her theory in the face of its obvious uselessness in solving the crime becomes the comic relief, like Inspector Lestrade in the Sherlock Holmes stories. Unfortunately, an educator who clings to a theory that is not helpful provides little humor for him- or herself or for others involved in the problem.

Problems as Mysteries: Educators as Sleuths

Thinking of a chronic problem as a mystery to be solved can help transform your role in the problem situation, metaphorically, from that of a salesperson for a point of view or a particular behavior to that of a competent detective puzzled by an intriguing case. In chronic problem situations, a salesperson inevitably finds her- or himself in a struggle. If the other people involved do not "buy" the salesperson's point of view, there is little guidance about what to do differently. The salesperson can try to bully, cajole, trick, manipulate, or bribe the others into buying her or his point of view or can accept defeat. In contrast, for a sleuth, the demolition of one theory helps provide additional information about how to construct a more useful one. The process of constructing and trying out new theories continues until the "case" is solved. It goes without saying that some cases will be tougher than others. But as you know from mystery fiction, detective heros love the tough cases most of all.

   Questions to Ask. As a sleuth, you will need to raise questions that provide you with clues about the ecosystemic relationships that are relevant to the problem you want to solve. A number of general questions will help you begin to consider the problem from an ecosystemic perspective. For example: What is the pattern that keeps repeating itself in this situation? How do the various people involved perceive the behavior in question? What are positive ways of interpreting the problem behavior? What would be a sign that things are on the way to getting better? What will this room, school, or playground be like when the problem behavior has stopped? What is happening in the situation that I do not want to change? The answers to questions such as these provide information you can use to reorient yourself toward the problem, thus setting the stage for you to use the techniques explained in Part Two.

Clues to Look For. In addition to raising questions intended to help you see the problem as part of an ecosystemic pattern, you should also look for clues that reveal how the others in the problem situation perceive what is happening. The best sources of clues are likely to be a person's figurative language and information about his or her interests and activities, which can be used metamorphically to communicate in the problem situation. When, for example, a student shouts at a teacher, "The classroom rules are driving me up the wall!" the teacher can use the student's phrase to inquire, "What sort of changes in the classroom would help you come down the wall again?" It is less important in instances such as this that the teacher know exactly what the student means by "the classroom rules are driving me up the wall" than that the teacher note, accept, and use the student's figurative expressions in talking with the student. Doing so will often enable people to reveal more clearly how the problem looks from their point of view, and it will help you see ways to change your usual way of talking with them about problems.

In the following case example, the teacher used her knowledge of three boys' involvement in a community football team to help her talk with them more effectively about a problem.

Case Example: The Quarterback Sneak

When students arrived at school in the morning, they had to decide whether to remain outdoors or to report to their first-hour class for quiet study time. The reason is that the school buses arrive at 8:25 A.M., and middle school classes first begin at 8:45 A.M. Unfortunately, students very often reported to their first-hour class with the idea of using the time for socializing rather than studying.

My first hour is a reading class; the students are sixth-graders who are homogeneously grouped and who are reading below grade level. During the regular class time, this group participated well in the class activities and were most cooperative. During the time period before class (8:25 A.M. to 8:45 A.M.), three boys, George, Tyrone, and Henry, usually came into the room, sat down, and began to carry on a loud conversation, while the other students worked quietly.

I usually found it necessary to remind the boys of the school rule, which temporarily settled them down. However, a short time later they would again be conversing loudly, until I threatened to keep them after school or keep them in during the lunch hour, which would end the situation.

In addition to assigning time after school or during the lunch hour, I had attempted a variety of ways of solving the problem. This included talking to the boys individually and suggesting that they simply remain outside if they wanted to talk and meeting them at the doorway and reminding them about an assignment they could review. I had even put extra-credit "mind teasers" on the board for them.

The idea of using an ecosystemic approach appealed to me, since it would enable me to stop resorting to threats or punishments to change the boys' behavior. Therefore, I decided that when the three boys entered my room, I would say, "Since you fellows seem to enjoy talking to one another, you will be able to use the back table for talking quietly when you first come in. When you are finished, then you may go to your seats and begin to work."

For the first few days the boys thought this was a great routine and followed it well. By the third day, however, they reverted to their previous behavior. In response, I decided to approach them individually. I said to Henry that I noticed how all the guys seemed to enjoy each others' company and got along very well. He volunteered the information that they were members of a community football team and that Tyrone was the quarterback.

The following day when Tyrone came in, I said to him, "You always seem to know what you are going to do in the morning, Tyrone, and you get right to it almost like you were running a football play." Each day I varied the phrasing (for example, "There you go again, knowing exactly what you are going to do"), until I reached a point where I was asking Tyrone, "What is your plan of attack today?" After his response, I would comment, "Sounds like it might just work."

Each day Tyrone began with doing something quiet. His involvement in the loud conversations dwindled. I said nothing about the talking situation. Eventually, after about four days, Tyrone *motioned* to George to join him at the portable reading machine. The two began practicing vocabulary review quietly! I decided not to comment on this event but to continue making statements to Tyrone each morning. During this time, Henry would come in and sit down quietly but do no work. He just watched his two friends. Occasionally he would call out a loud comment to them, which they usually ignored.

As the days went by, I began making comments to Henry such as "it's tough to be on the sidelines when you want to be in on the action" or "sometimes the guys on the sidelines do a little practicing too."

Henry comes in and sits down quietly for longer periods of time now. He works on study materials for a while and then reverts to his loud questions or comments to others. But now the comments are directed toward other individuals. It seems his behavior has changed, whether he wanted it to or not. I will continue to monitor and intervene.

As a result of my "talking their language," two of the boys, Tyrone and George, are working in an acceptable manner. This situation has shown me not only that it is helpful to describe behavior in a positive manner but also that you must be able to communicate this in terms that are meaningful to the people involved. Had I not initiated the original positive statement to George, I would not have known of the close football ties these boys shared. I also learned that it is unimportant to me who is in charge or "calling the shots," as long as the job gets done. As events, student experiences, and student behaviors change, new interventions will be needed. I realize this is an ongoing process.

Noticing Changes

After you have begun trying to solve your "case," you must be alert to any changes that are occurring. Obviously, you will notice any hoped-for change in the problem behavior. You may not, however, notice other positive changes if your attention is focused only on the problem behavior. Noticing positive changes will serve as a source of encouragement and help make it easier to consider solutions that may be different than the particular solution you had originally imagined. It is surprising how many changes you will see when you look for them.

In the following case example, a number of changes occurred before the problem was solved. These changes occurred in a very short period of time, were clearly related to each other, and seemed to prepare the way for the result the teacher wanted.

Case Example: Distant Drums

My sixth-period class had been giving me a lot of trouble. There are thirty-five boys in the class. About ten of them caused most of the problems. One thing they did that really bothered me was that all ten of them would tap their desk tops in unison with their fingers. Yelling, threats, and a variety of punishments failed to stop this noisemaking. The boys' drumming really frustrated me and interfered with my teaching.

Because I had little to lose, I decided to try to use positive connotation. (Positive-connotation techniques are described in Chapters Five and Six.) One day when the tapping began, I stopped lecturing (change 1) and listened attentively (change 2) to the drummers for about a minute. I then told them that I appreciated their "love of music" (change 3) and thanked them for sharing their "talents" with the rest of the class (change 4). I also told them that their drumming provided a nice background to my lecture (change 5).

I do not know exactly why or how, but I was able to say what I said sincerely. Anyway, just as I had feared, everyone started tapping on their desk tops (change 6). What happened next surprised me. Suddenly we all laughed (change 7), and the tapping stopped (change 8). After that incident, every time the noise started up, I repeated my statement about the drummers' "love of music" (change 9). Only one or two students would begin to tap, and they would stop as soon as I began to say something (change 10).

The "Distant Drums" case example illustrates how in problem situations many changes may occur before a satisfactory solution is reached. However, problems in schools and classrooms often do not resolve themselves as neatly as in this example. Frequently changes are widely spaced, are seemingly unrelated, and do not seem to contribute to the outcome you had hoped for. In these instances, it is easy not to notice the changes because they are not perceived as solutions or as contributing to a solution. Nevertheless, it is important to notice them.

The following case example illustrates how many different changes occurred as the problem situation evolved. Unlike in the "Distant Drums" case example, this teacher's success was neither immediate nor complete.

Case Example: The Talker

Betzadia is a seventh-grade girl whose talking would begin as soon as she entered my classroom. When class had started, and the other students were exchanging papers and notebooks to correct, Betzadia would talk. When the other students were ready to begin correcting their work, I read the answers out loud. Inevitably Betzadia would yell, "Wait!" as she scrambled to get her materials ready. Even after she had organized herself, it would be only a matter of seconds before she began talking again. I would then say, "Betzadia, pay attention to the paper you are supposed to be correcting." This, as well as a few other reprimands, would usually stop her talking for anywhere from two to five minutes.

When her talking resumed, my warnings would take on a more serious and direct tone. I would say, for example, "Betzadia, stop your talking now!" In search of a defense, she often responded, "Well, she asked me a question," or, "He's calling me names." The end result was that I usually ordered everyone to be quiet.

Disciplining Betzadia for talking had become a regular part of my classroom routine. The students seemed accustomed to this daily disciplining ritual. At times, those sitting close to Betzadia would turn toward her and, in not-so-polite terms, tell her to "shut up!"

Everything I had tried so far had not worked. I decided to attempt to use ecosystemic techniques in order to help change the disruptive behavior. I planned to follow a three-step strategy. First, I would let Betzadia know how much I admire the great emphasis she places on friendship (as evidenced by her willingness to risk poor grades in order to nurture her friendship by talking). Second, I would help her classmates understand that, even though at times her talking disturbs them, she is also helping us all learn how to cope in a world filled with distractions. Finally, if needed, I would ask that Betzadia continue to strengthen her friendship, but in a way that does not distract the rest of the class. She and her friend would have to write notes to each other.

I was enthusiastic about putting my plan into operation. Sure enough, just like clockwork, soon after class began on Monday, Betzadia began chatting. Overlooking this talking, I waited until she became entangled in a problem caused by her own negligence (change 1). It was not too much later when this happened. It was Betzadia's turn to answer; she did not know it was her turn, and when her classmates told her to go, she did not know which question we were on, since she had been "preoccupied."

"Betzadia," I began (I could see the class was already expecting another reprimanding lecture directed at her), "in the past, I have often become rather angry when you were talking, but I guess I failed to realize just how important friendship is to you. The fact is that you risk doing poorly in school in order to preserve your friendship with Connie. Perhaps, for some people, friendship must sometimes come before grades. I can respect your attitude" (change 2). I tried as hard as possible to speak in all sincerity, because I did not want Betzadia or the rest of the class to get the impression that I was being sarcastic.

At first, the kids began to snicker as I started talking. They thought this was going to be another of my attempts at humor. But as they sensed my seriousness, they became attentive. As I finished, many had puzzled looks on their faces as they turned toward each other (change 3). Had Mr. Collins finally gone off the deep end?

Betzadia, apparently also expecting a lecture, had a similarly puzzled expression on her face but quickly retorted, "Yea" (change 4), as her classmates turned to observe her reaction to my comment. While she did talk briefly a few times after this, she remained mostly quiet for the rest of the period (change 5). As the students left the class that day, you could hear bits and pieces of mumbled disbelief (change 6).

The next day, Betzadia's talking resumed. I tried my best to ignore it (change 7). As some nearby students became annoyed with her talking, some responded rather sarcastically, "She's building her friendship" (change 8). Knowing that I was quickly losing the faith of the rest of the class, I swiftly put my second strategy into play. I explained to the class that Betzadia was helping us to survive in a world filled with distractions (change 9), and if they found the distraction unbearable, they should feel free to move (change 10), at which point some did (change 11). Some students seemed to prefer this response, since it treated Betzadia like a force of nature. Betzadia smugly replied, "Yea." While she did engage in some talking, it was much more limited (change 12). I treated her as a natural disturbance also and tried to put her and her talking out of my mind (change 13).

Betzadia's limited talking continued for the better part of the week. The next week, however, the original problem of excessive talking resurfaced (change 14). It was time to implement my third strategy. Telling Betzadia that I was keeping both her interests and those of her classmates in mind, I said that when she felt the compelling need to talk, she should write down what she had to say in note form, carry it over to Connie, and have Connie write her response and return it to Betzadia (change 15). After all, this was English class. Again, the students' puzzled looks reappeared. Betzadia seemed raring to go. She scribbled something down in her notebook, folded it, and carried it over to Connie (change 16). Connie was less eager to participate, however, and never returned Betzadia's message.

The next day, when Betzadia began talking, I reminded her of her duty to send the note. Again she cooperatively followed through. Connie responded this time, but only once (change 17). When Betzadia tried to contact Connie again verbally, I simply pointed in Betzadia's direction to communicate that she should use the notebook (change 18).

While some communicating continued, most of it was one-sided—Betzadia as the sender (change 19). The next day, the students asked if they too could use this system (change 20). Trying to downplay the strategy as much as possible, I continued with the lesson (change 21).

While Betzadia's talking has been reduced (change 22), it does occasionally happen. The messenger service is used sparingly, but now I must remember not to let this become a new distracting behavior for me (change 23).

The changes in the behavior of the teacher and the students and the changes in the teacher's and students' attitudes in "The Talker" case example are inseparable. Those changes reshaped the classroom ecosystem and transformed the problem situation. In this instance, the problem behavior did not completely disappear. However, it was modified. Also, the teacher's attitude toward the situation changed enough so that Betzadia's behavior was no longer as much of a distraction for him as it had been previously.

Finally, although the teacher does not comment on it, his ability to notice and respond to changes as they occurred helped him to keep things from returning to their problematic pattern. In problem situations, recognizing changes helps promote constructive solutions, because seeing these changes helps to shed new light on the problem situation and the people in it. A good sleuth learns to look for, and sometimes comment on, changes, even changes that have nothing directly to do with the problem, as a way of positively influencing problem behavior patterns.

The Importance of Humor

If you smiled at times while reading our characterization of educators in problem situations as sleuths, you have experienced another important aspect of translating ecosystemic concepts into methods—humor. People in chronic problem situations tend to find those situations anything but humorous. Chronic problems are often described with negative imagery that ranges in intensity from annoying (the problem is like a knot in a shoelace: the harder you pull, the tighter it gets) to quite frightening (the problem is like quicksand: the more fiercely you struggle to be free, the faster you descend). It is often the very seriousness with which a problem is viewed that inhibits the flexibility of thought and the creativity that are so helpful in changing things. The ability to find the humor in a situation that had previously produced only clenched teeth and a knotted stomach is a big change and is often enough, in itself, to influence events positively. Perhaps this is why the case examples of educators who have used ecosystemic techniques often have a certain lightheartedness in common.

Finding a positive alternative description of a problem behavior or acting differently in a problem situation helps place the problem in a new perspective. Perhaps finding a new perspective on an old problem removes some of the melodrama from the situation and helps make it possible for a person to smile once again. Perhaps being able to smile about a problem makes it possible to find new perspectives. Which comes first probably does not matter. What does seem clear is that feeling positively makes a difference. In an exhaustive review of the literature entitled "Illusion and Well-Being: A Social Psychological Perspective on Mental Health," Taylor and Brown (1988) write that what they characterize as "positive illusions" "may promote the capacity for creative, productive work in two ways: First, these illusions may facilitate intellectually creative functioning itself; second, they enhance motivation, persistence and performance" (p. 198). They go on to say that "positive affect facilitates unusual and diverse associations which may produce more creative problem-solving" (pp. 198–199).

The Use of Paradox

The techniques described in the following chapters are generally referred to in the family therapy literature as paradoxical techniques. This literature contains numerous descriptions of paradoxical strategies (see, for example, Greenberg, 1973; Fay, 1978; Bogdan, 1982; Weeks and L'Abate, 1982; Weeks, 1985; and Seltzer, 1986). These descriptions are sometimes complex and technical. For our purposes, the definition offered by the unabridged edition of the

Random House Dictionary of the English Language (1971) will do quite nicely. Paradox is defined as "a statement or proposition seemingly self-contradictory or absurd but in reality expressing a possible truth" (p. 1046).

From an ecosystemic perspective, chronic problem situations are characterized by the stability of the points of view and behavior of the people involved. Since a person's commonsense view of things is the product of complex and profound social interactions that have occurred over a relatively long time, that view is rarely susceptible to change by direct confrontation. Paradoxical techniques are powerful because they do not attack the commonsense view; instead, they allow other views to "grow up" alongside it.

Paradoxical techniques are an effective way of representing the ecosystemic view that in any situation many things can be true at the same time and of doing so without requiring that previously held beliefs be labeled as false. Paradoxical techniques are used to introduce new interpretations into problem situations. These new interpretations may often seem contradictory or even absurd. However, in fact, they are straightforward representations of a different perspective on the situations or behaviors considered problematic.

Paradoxical techniques can also be used to change behavior and events seemingly unrelated to the problem and thus influence the problem situation. If you think about the problem situation as part of a larger pattern of ecosystemic relationships, one way of solving the problem is, paradoxically, to concentrate on those aspects of the person or the situation that are not problematic. The usefulness of focusing on the nonproblem parts of the ecosystem in order to change problem behaviors has been described by family therapists (de Shazer and others, 1986; Molnar and de Shazer, 1987) and has also been demonstrated in school examples (see Chapters Eight and Nine).

Putting Ecosystemic Techniques in Perspective

When you read through the description of ecosystemic techniques in Part Two, it would not be surprising if you find that you can explain one or more of them from a familiar perspective. In discussing family therapy methods, Duhl and Duhl (1981) contend that the same intervention can be interpreted from a variety of perspectives. Jaynes and Rugg (1988) argue that having a parent "take charge" through setting clear limits and consequences can be equally well explained using either a structural or a behavioral rationale. The most likely alternative way of characterizing an ecosystemic approach in therapy is as a behavioral approach. Chambless and Goldstein (1979) describe behavioral psychotherapy as a treatment system that draws on the work of Wolpe (behavior therapy) and Skinner (behavior modification). Within this broad category, a number of methods that seem consonant with an ecosystemic approach are used. For example, the work of Ellis (1962), Beck (1967), Stuart (1969), Hawkins, Peterson, Schweid, and Bijou (1971), Patterson (1971), and Mahoney (1974) leads to clinical practices that at times may look very similar to the ecosystemic techniques described in Part Two.

You may find that some of our case examples remind you of reinforcement (Skinner, 1968), Adlerian (Dreikurs, 1968), cognitive-behavior modification (Meichenbaum, 1977), attribution theory (Nisbett and Ross, 1980), behavior management (Wielkiewicz, 1986), or motivation theory (Wlodkowski, 1986a, 1986b) approaches to changing problem behavior in schools. It would be natural for you to try to understand how ecosystemic techniques work by using a theoretical perspective with which you are already familiar. However, although the ecosystemic approach we are describing is not well developed enough to lay claim to sharply defined conceptual boundaries, we do not think it will be helpful for you to try and understand ecosystemic techniques in terms of a way of explaining problem behavior that you find more familiar. The risk is that, if you do so, you will actually strengthen a way of characterizing a chronic problem behavior that has already proven unhelpful to you and misuse the ecosystemic technique you want to employ by trying to make it conform to the rules imposed by another approach to changing behavior.

There may be situations in which you may not wish to use ecosystemic techniques or in which ecosystemic techniques should be used as part of a larger plan. In schools, crisis situations sometimes arise that must be responded to immediately. Experienced therapists use systemic techniques in crisis situations, and experienced educators have successfully used the ideas presented in this book in situations that required a quick response. In this book, however, we are not attempting to teach you how to use these methods in crisis situations. Rather, we are recommending the use of these techniques in chronic problem situations in which the problematic behavior and response to it are predictable.

There are also situations in schools that must be dealt with in prescribed ways owing to federal, state, and local laws or school policy. For example, in Wisconsin, educators are required by law to report child abuse. Ecosystemic ideas are to be used in addition to, not instead of, such mandated requirements. Even after an educator has reported the abuse, he or she must still work with the child in the school setting. The suggestions in this book are intended to help school personnel in their daily or weekly contacts with the student that continue even after a report has been filed or some other required procedure has been implemented.

Finally, there are times when it is appropriate to refer students and their families for therapy. We are not suggesting that educators become psychotherapists. However, despite an appropriate referral for therapy, school personnel must still work with students in the school setting. The ideas presented in this book can be helpful in working with students within the context of the school and classroom.

Changing Yourself: You Are the Expert

For people who are experiencing a problem, recognition of an intellectual reason to change is very often not sufficient to change either their point of view or their behavior. Family therapists know that family members often blame their family's problem on each other. Each family member tends to expect some other family member to change to solve the problem. Family therapists, therefore, focus their initial efforts to help the family resolve their problem on the person who seems to be experiencing the most pain as a result of the problem, not necessarily on the person the family may have identified as "the problem." This way of approaching problems can also help educators change their behavior in problem situations.

In a problem situation, the discomfort experienced by a teacher, school psychologist, counselor, social worker, or principal, for example, helps provide a reason for thinking and acting differently. Furthermore, although an educator may have little direct control over the ideas and behaviors of others, the educator does have a significant amount of control over her or his own thoughts and behavior. This being the case, it is easier for the educator, as the person who experiences the problem, to change her or his thinking or behavior as a way of encouraging change in a chronic problem situation than it is for the educator to change someone else's behavior or thinking.

Although this seems like a straightforward proposition, it is not unusual for educators to think about changing the ideas or behavior of the problem person while tacitly assuming that they themselves will remain the same. Classrooms and schools are ecosystems, and one person cannot remain the same while others change, because all perceptions and behaviors in the ecosystem interact with and influence each other. In order to try reframing, positive connotation, symptom prescription, or any of the other techniques in the following chapters, you will, of necessity, change your perception of the problem and your behavior in relation to it. Thus, the techniques explained in Part Two are methods of helping you change your ideas about and your behavior in relation to a chronic problem you want to solve. In this way, they are also methods of influencing the behavior of another person.

As we mentioned in Chapter Two, ecosystemic techniques do not require that you adopt a new style or learn a new vocabulary. To start putting ecosystemic ideas to work, all you need to do is decide that it is time to try something new in a problem situation. It will be easier for you to make this decision if you are sure that you will not solve the problem by doing what you already know how to do. Since you are the expert on your problem and on yourself, you know what you will and will not attempt. You know the other people in the situation. You know what you have already tried. You know the demands and expectations of your school. You are a professional paid to make professional judgments. Although ecosystemic ideas have been used very successfully in a variety of problem situations, the decision to use any of our ideas in a problem situation you face is a matter of your professional judgment.

Finally, and perhaps most important, if and when you use the techniques described in this book, you will want to be sure that you are convinced that you can use them honestly and sincerely. Since ecosystemic techniques ignore the commonsense "truth" about a problem situation, some people initially confuse ecosystemic techniques with "reverse psychology" (saying one thing and thinking something else in order to trick another person into doing what you want) and suspect that they are somehow dishonest. This is an issue that you will also have to confront. From an ecosystemic perspective, there are many truths about any behavior. Many ecosystemic techniques are simply ways of finding and acting on a different truth in a problem situation in order to change it.

If, in any problem situation, you find that you cannot honestly describe the behavior or the situation in a new way, then you should not attempt to use ecosystemic techniques. These techniques are not mind games used for saying one thing while thinking another. Reverse psychology is best left to Tom Sawyer. As you read the descriptions of the techniques in Part Two, remember that there is no substitute for your personal and professional judgment when considering whether it is appropriate for you to use ecosystemic ideas to help you solve a problem that just will not go away.

4

Thinking Differently About the Problem

In Chapter One, we explained that it is difficult to change behavior in problem situations because, although people's behavior and their perceptions of behavior may be in conflict, they are related elements of stable, self-reinforcing patterns of social interaction. Consider a simple example. A teacher regards a student's repeated blurting out of answers during class as an unreasonable and inappropriate attempt to get attention; the student considers it necessary to blurt out answers because he or she believes that the teacher tends to ignore him or her. The teacher and the student each have their perceptions reinforced when the student blurts out to get the teacher's attention and the teacher determinedly ignores the student in an attempt to discourage the behavior. The relationship between the behavior of the student and the behavior of the teacher is only a small element in the complex pattern of relationships that constitutes the classroom ecosystem. It is of interest because it is problematic. From an ecosystemic perspective, we know that any change in the exchange between the teacher and student in our example will necessarily influence the classroom ecosystem, and vice versa. The question is, of course, how do we encourage constructive change?

The Reframing Technique

Family therapists who have adopted what we call an ecosystemic perspective have found that one powerful way of promoting change in problematic patterns of behavior is to formulate a positive

45

alternative interpretation of the problem behavior and to encourage their clients to introduce this interpretation into the problem situation by acting in ways that are consistent with it. This technique is called reframing.

For an educator, reframing means finding a new perceptual "frame" for problem behavior, one that is positive, fits the facts of the situation, and is plausible to the people involved. A reframing will also suggest how to act differently in the problem situation. If the teacher in our example were able to interpret the student's blurting out answers as intense involvement and interest in his lessons instead of as inappropriate attempts to get attention, then responses other than ignoring the student would suggest themselves.

If a problem behavior in school is viewed as part of a self-reinforcing ecosystemic pattern, then it follows that a change in your perception of that behavior will help reshape the social context of the problem and thus influence the problem behavior. In a school setting, the first change in the social context will be in the perception and behavior of the person doing the reframing. This is somewhat different than in a therapeutic setting. In therapy a therapist offers reframings to which family members respond. In a school setting, an educator who wishes to use reframing must formulate the reframing and alter his or her behavior to be consistent with it. It will help you to understand and use the technique of reframing if you are familiar with and accept the propositions discussed in Chapter Three. Those propositions are (1) that many interpretations of a given behavior can be true at the same time and (2) that a person's behavior (including the behavior you consider problematic) will be regarded by that person as an appropriate response to the situation as he or she perceives it. If you are not clear about these points, you may want to review Chapter Three before proceeding.

Analysis of Case Examples

Throughout each of the following case examples, we have provided explanatory comments to underscore the key elements of reframing. For example, in the case example below, one way of interpreting the boys' behavior is that they are purposely trying to make life difficult for their teacher. Another interpretation is that they are trying to get out of doing their work. A positive interpretation of the boys' behavior is that they are very good friends who want to reaffirm their bond of friendship each morning by talking with each other. When the teacher explained the students' behavior to herself as the boys' willful attempt to make trouble for her, she responded accordingly, and the chronic problem continued. When the teacher reframed the situation (that is, focused on a positive alternative interpretation of the boys' behavior and acted based on this new interpretation), she altered the pattern of interaction that had defined the chronic problem situation. By focusing on a positive interpretation of the boys' behavior, the teacher changed her perception of the problem behavior and was therefore able to change the way she responded to it. From an ecosystemic perspective, by changing her behavior, she necessarily influenced the boys' behavior.

Case Example: Lazy Troublemakers or Best Friends?

Bob insisted on spending as much time as possible out of his seat standing next to Pete. They are best friends, and they help each other with everything. For example, when one answers a question, the other says, "Yes, that's right."

Every morning the children came into the room, sat down, and performed some small task quietly while I collected the lunch money. They were held accountable for doing this morning work as reinforcement.

Every morning Bob came in and stood next to Pete's desk, and they would talk about the events of the previous evening. I told Bob repeatedly to take his seat, because it was difficult to see around him and to hear the responses of the other children while I collected lunch money. Also, since Bob was talking to Pete, he did not complete the morning work. In the past it had taken three or four pleasant requests and one more threatening request for Bob finally to go to his seat, where he would still talk or flash messages to Pete. At this point I was usually irate, Pete and Bob did not have their work done, and because of all the confusion, the lunch count was off.

I decided to try reframing. My interpretation of the problem had been that Pete and Bob were trying to waste time, get out of doing their work, and cause a rough time for me. [The teacher's interpretation of the meaning of the boys' behavior had been negative, that is, that they were trying to waste time, get out of doing their work, and cause a rough time for her.] In thinking about the situation, I came up with another explanation of their behavior. My positive alternative interpretation was that Bob and Pete were good friends who wanted to spend time together first thing every morning as a way of affirming their bond of friendship. [As this teacher applies reframing, she begins to consider positive alternative ways of interpreting the students' behavior. Having found a plausible positive alternative explanation for their behavior, she formulates a statement she can say to them using this new interpretation, and she acts based on it.]

The next morning when Bob came in and stood at Pete's desk, I said, "Bob, I think it is really great to see that you have such a strong friendship with Pete that you want to spend time with him every morning." He looked at me, raised his arms, and said, "Okay, okay. I'm going to my seat." He obviously did not think I was serious.

The next morning, as Bob stood next to Pete's desk and began talking, I said, "Bob, you go right ahead and spend some time with Pete; sometimes a strong friendship is more important than anything else." He looked at me as though I was being sarcastic, and Pete began to giggle. As I maintained my matter-of-fact composure, their doubt turned to amazement. [In creating a reframing, it is important that the positive interpretation be plausible to everyone involved. In order for this teacher to say the reframing honestly and not sarcastically, it had to be plausible to her, and in order for the students to take it seriously, it had to be plausible to them.] Bob spoke to Pete only about fifteen seconds more and went to his seat and completed his work.

Bob still stops at Pete's desk to chat for two to three minutes each morning, but then he goes to his seat and begins his work. He is getting more work done. I am starting the day in a much better mood, and I find myself being more tolerant of all my students.

Discussion. The process this teacher went through illustrates some of the essentials of reframing. She identified the negative interpretations she had applied to the problem behavior. She thought the situation through and developed a positive alternative interpretation for the problem behavior, one that was plausible to her so she could say the reframing honestly and not sarcastically. She chose an interpretation that was plausible to the students so they would take her new positive interpretation seriously.

This case example also demonstrates that it is sometimes necessary to repeat a reframing. Handling a problem situation using reframing leads one to act in very different ways and to say quite different things to the other person or persons in the problem situation. It is not uncommon for the listener, on first hearing a reframing, to be a bit taken aback. For this reason it may be necessary to repeat the reframing in order for the listener to grasp it.

Finally, this teacher's concluding comments illustrate the affective and behavioral changes that take place as a result of using reframing and their ecosystemic implications, "He is getting more work done. I am starting the day in a much better mood, and I find myself being more tolerant of all my students."

The Sunday school teacher in the next case example began to describe one of her students with problem behavior as a hard worker needing a break instead of as a disruptive influence. Her ability to adopt a cooperative perspective (to consider how the situation might look to the student) helped her to reframe the student's behavior and allowed both of them to behave differently.

Case Example: Disruptive Devil or Hardworking Angel?

After successfully using reframing in my classroom, I decided to try my newfound skill on a student in my Sunday school class. I have the students for two years, and Todd had been quite a handful since last year. He usually arrived in class with a flourish, talking loudly, bugging the other students, asking when we were having the snack, and most of all complaining about doing the class work. During the lesson, he often continued these antics. Sometimes I had the unchristian wish that he would not show up on Sunday.

In the past, I had tried the usual methods of dealing with this type of child. I had ignored him, scolded him, and threatened him. I had used the usual types of bribes, such as stickers, food, and games. Nothing seemed to be effective over any period of time.

Last Sunday, when Todd arrived for Sunday school, he came in his usual manner, loud and demanding. On the spot I reframed his behavior. I calmly put my arm around him and told him that it was understandable if he felt it was unfair that he had to get up early for Sunday school. I told him I knew he worked hard in school all week, and now he had to do more work. [The Sunday school teacher begins to describe the problem situation in the way it might seem to the student, that is, that he works hard all week in school, and now he has to do more work. Given this perspective, instead of trying to get him to behave in Sunday school, she proposes an alternative.]

I said it would be fine with me if he wanted to rejoin his family up in church for the service. Then he would not have to do any work. [The Sunday school teacher does not know why Todd has been acting in the way he has. She knows he has complained about the Sunday school work, and she knows he attends school during the week. Using a cooperative perspective (that is, recognizing that the situation may look different from Todd's perspective and that, given his interpretation of the situation, he will regard his behavior as reasonable), she looks for a positive interpretation of his behavior that takes his perspective into account and does not blame him for the problem. By describing Todd as a hard worker and suggesting that perhaps he is even overworked and needs a break, the teacher changes the way she has previously thought about and interacted with Todd. This change in her behavior allows him the opportunity to change, too.] I said the pastor would probably be impressed with his interest in listening to the sermon instead of attending Sunday school. As I started to walk him back out of the classroom, I genuinely believed that Todd might really prefer the sermon. But all of a sudden he stopped dead in his tracks and looked up at me. He asked, if he did not enjoy being up in church, could he come back to Sunday school? I assured him that it would be fine with me. He took a few more steps, then said he would rather stay in Sunday school. He came into the classroom and worked like a trouper. He has returned the last two Sundays, and although I can still hear him coming, when he enters the classroom, he settles down with a minimum amount of talking and complaining.

Discussion. Why did Todd's behavior change? Consider the difference between being ignored, scolded, threatened, and bribed and being told you are a hard worker who deserves a break. By reframing Todd's behavior and describing him as a hard worker, the teacher created a new situation that was different from the problem situation. In the problem situation, Todd was described as and acted like a disruptive student. In the new situation, created by the teacher's new interpretation of his behavior, Todd is considered a hard worker who deserves a break. Todd the hard worker was always there, and the teacher, on seeing Todd the hard worker, helped create him.

Acting toward a person based on what one believes to be true about that person tends to strengthen that aspect or truth and to create that reality. For example, in Rosenthal and Jacobson's well-known work, described in *Pygmalion in the Classroom* (1968), teachers "saw" and helped create "intellectual bloomers" from students without any particular intellectual promise.

The teacher in the next case example was able to cooperate with the student, and together they created a helpful student from a disruptive one.

Case Example: The Miracle Workers

Judith is a five-year-old kindergarten student who pushed and shoved everyone out of line in order to be first every time the children lined up. All the children were given turns to be first, but Judith thought she should be first all the time.

I had talked to Judith about taking turns and being fair. I also had let her stand second in the line, and if the pushing and shoving continued, she was put at the end of the line. None of these attempts was successful. Judith continued this unacceptable behavior.

I decided to reframe the situation. I had seen Judith's behavior as unfair to the other students and disruptive for me. As I began to look at things differently, I realized that, unlike some of the other children, who dawdled and had to be told several times to line up, Judith was always right there immediately after I would tell the children to line up. I decided I could use this kind of enthusiasm, so Judith became my "line helper." I posted a list of all the children's names and gave Judith the job of choosing the leader and printing his or her name on the chalkboard. As soon as that child had been given a turn to be the leader, Judith crossed out her or his name, so that every child in the class, including Judith, was given a turn. Each day Judith and I had a little chat about how the line moved in the halls and out to the playground.

A miracle happened. Judith took to this plan like a duck to water. She is now choosing the leader and printing the name on the chalkboard, which is an added bonus, as she is getting much needed practice in printing. She is cooperating very well, coming along at the end of the line so she can watch all the children. Our little chats are giving her some extra attention. Everything is working well.

I guess in this situation the reframing was as much for me as for the student, because I did not actually say anything to her about my new way of looking at things. I just started working with her differently.

Discussion. The teacher in this case example notes that the reframing was as much for her as for the student. All reframings have their initial effect on the person formulating the reframing. It is this new perceptual frame that allows them to say and do things differently.

This case is interesting because, unlike most of the other case examples, the teacher does not attempt to say anything to the student that reflects the reframing. Rather, the teacher lets the reframing speak through the actions she takes.

As the next case study illustrates, successfully reframing a student's behavior in a specific problem situation may have a ripple effect that spills over into other academic areas and may even influence the entire teacher-student relationship.

Case Example: Belligerent Bad Guy or Awkward Adolescent?

As a sixth-grade teacher, I have witnessed numerous ways in which students attempt to assume leadership roles and increase their popularity. Many students rise due to their academic or verbal abilities, while others rely more on their appearance or athletic skills. Some others, because of their physical maturity, tower over their peers and are able to demand a following rather than earn one.

Such was the case in my sixth-grade class this year. Rick has towered over his classmates since the primary grades. He is a sixth-grader who could easily pass for a high school senior. His physical stature has provided him easy dominance over the others. Rather than becoming a partner in the classroom, Rich assumed an "anti-authority" position as a tough guy or rebel. Throughout the school year, he tried to live up to his image by not completing assignments, not participating in regular classroom activities, distracting teachers, and intimidating other students. [The negative interpretations the teacher has of this student's behavior are obviously not casually drawn; they suggest that the teacher has used his experience with other students in the past as well as his knowledge about this particular student in his classroom and elsewhere in the school to create a rather complex understanding of the student's behavior. He takes into account the student's size and how he perceives the student using it. And he interprets the student's not participating or doing his assignments as demonstrating his being a rebel. As discussed in Chapter One, sometimes previous knowledge, experience, and social support for a particular interpretation of problem behavior can make it difficult to search for alternative, especially positive, interpretations. Teachers as well as other educators are likely to be under considerable peer pressure not to change their behavior in a way that their colleagues might regard as "giving in" or "lowering standards." This can make the task of reframing more difficult and may require more effort to use a cooperative perspective and search for positive interpretations of problem behavior on the part of the educator.]

At the beginning of the school year, I tried to draw Rick into my favor by assigning him special duties that I hoped would encourage positive leadership. Many of those small assignments were manipulated and mismanaged and turned against me. I have tried to talk with Rick, letting him know my expectations of him. I have told him that I expected him at least to respect my desire to have a safe and proper educational environment for others. Rick seemed to enjoy the fact that he was an effective disrupter. Many times, feeling up against the wall, I met Rick squarely and confronted his aggression with my own, threatening him with detentions and suspension. This only strengthened his image. [The teacher describes clearly how his perceptions and actions and those of the student interact not only to maintain but at times to strengthen the problem situation.]

Just recently, the students in my class were preparing for a musical that would be presented to the school and the parents. Rick's desire not to participate in such "dumb stuff" seemed to be rubbing off on others. I needed to do something, so I thought I would try reframing. [In order to reframe the student's behavior, the teacher must abandon his previous interpretation of Rick's behavior as rebellious, antiauthority, and so on and find a new, nonnegative interpretation that is plausible to both the teacher and Rick. Acting consistently with this new interpretation leads to a different way of responding to the student.]

During a rehearsal in which the students were practicing hand movements to a song and Rick was acting silly, I walked over to him and told him that I could appreciate his discomfort in participating. As an adult about his size, I, too, felt awkward in trying to do the activities. I invited him to feel free to step aside and just watch, as I was doing.

Rick seemed a bit taken aback. He did not participate for the rest of that period, but he also did not create any disruption. During our next rehearsal, I was surprised to see Rick make some serious attempts to join in with the rest of the class, and as the practice sessions continued, Rick's involvement became more serious.

It has been several weeks since I used the reframing. I have witnessed an attitude change in Rick with regard to not only his participation but also his attitude toward me. I have been able to talk to him about his work, and he seems to be more open to my ideas and suggestions. His work in the classroom is improving, although he has gotten into trouble in a few incidents outside of the room. I am very pleasantly surprised and impressed with the results of this technique.

Just this afternoon after school, Rick reentered the classroom after all the students had left and said, "Have a nice weekend." He has never before even said good-bye. I find this a really significant change.

Discussion. This case example illustrates how easily the interactions of people in problem situations can maintain and strengthen the problem. A concerned, sensitive teacher who had tried a variety of approaches still found himself at times confronting the student's aggression with his own. Fortunately, the teacher was willing to continue sleuthing until he had created a hypothesis that accounted for the facts of the student's behavior, offered a different interpretation of the meaning of the behavior, and suggested an alterative way of acting. His sleuthing was rewarded by rather dramatic changes in the problem situation after using the technique of reframing.

As was pointed out earlier in the chapter, reframing always has an effect on the person using the technique as well as on others in the problem situation. The following case example is particularly interesting, because one of the first changes that took place was the change in the teacher's perception. This case is also noteworthy because of the number of people who became involved in an effort to solve the problem.

Case Example: Sad Sarah—with Good Reason

The group of students I have this year is a challenge, to say the least. I have at a minimum four different problem students that I wanted to try reframing with, but I restrained myself and selected just one.

I will call this child Sad Sarah. The first day of the school year she came into my room crying. She would continue to cry until I would step in and ask her what the problem was. She would state some ailment such as a headache, stomachache, nausea, or the like. The crying upset the students at her table. The principal, the student coordinator, and the mother also were concerned. It really bothered me that so many people were upset at this child's crying each day. Sarah was quiet and shy. She was bright, and the work she turned in was of excellent caliber. I truly wanted to help her, but the constant crying outbursts were getting to me.

It seemed that as soon as Sarah sat at her table at 8:30 A.M., big tears would start rolling down her cheeks. I asked if she cried on the bus or the playground before school started. She would state that she did not. I would ask her what the problem was and try to cheer her up. When all else failed, I would send her to the office. The office would refer her to the nurse. Most of the time nothing physically wrong could be found. Several times Sarah was sent home. From day one, like clockwork, we went through the same pattern. In all my teaching experience, I had never seen a case quite like this one. I had had children who would cry, but never for this long. I was baffled.

At first I tried to solve the problem by talking to Sarah. I would ask questions about the nature of her sadness. I also tried to cheer her up. I told her things were not so bad and tried to point out positive things.

When the crying continued, I sent her to the office, because I thought she really might be sick. Her mother came and picked her up. After a week of this, the mother wanted to know what the problem was, so we set up a conference. We found out that the doctor had examined Sarah and found nothing wrong. Her mother was supportive. We decided to ignore the crying; needless to say, it escalated.

Next we involved the coordinator. Instead of having Sarah come into the classroom first, we had her go to the coordinator's room to do some artwork, in which she excels. We had the 8:30 crying under control, but this was not something that could go on all year. Besides, she would still start crying later in the morning or in the afternoon.

The principal sent me a note to see what progress we were making, and he made himself available to help.

A new student entered our class at the end of September. I assigned this child to Sarah's table in an attempt to divert attention to someone else. Sarah is a good student and knows what is going on in class; she could be of enormous help to the new child. Now we had her out of the coordinator's office in the morning, but she still cried later in the day. The mother was concerned that if this behavior continued, she would have to send Sarah back to her old school.

The art teacher also made a social worker referral about Sarah's behavior in the art room. Even with all this intervention,

I still had a crying, sad child in October. [Here is a teacher who has successfully solved problems with crying children in the past but who is stymied in this situation. She has been partially successful with this child by using what she already knows how to do and involving others, but, as she points out, the problem is still not solved. To this teacher's credit, she is willing to try something different instead of continuing to repeat interventions that have worked in the past but are not working in the current situation.]

It seemed to me reframing might help. I began to look at the situation from Sarah's point of view. I started to think about agreeing with her that it was understandable that she was sad. And, yes, she did miss her old school and her friends. I noticed that the more I thought in this way, the more my position in the case was changing. Instead of thinking about trying to cheer up Sarah, I was beginning to sympathize and understand her point of view.

The next Monday, before saying or doing anything, I just observed. I wanted to see what would happen. Sure enough, at 9:45 Sarah cried. On Wednesday I talked with her. I really listened. She stated that she missed her old school and the teachers and friends she had there. I also knew that she was a perfectionist and did not want any failure. I told her it was understandable that she missed her old school and felt sad about leaving it. I did not try to cheer her up or talk her out of being sad by pointing out the positive things in this new school. [Perhaps in the past pointing out positive things to students has helped cheer them up; it was not helping this student. The teacher's ability to reframe the situation and see it as the student saw it allowed her to say sincerely that it was understandable the child was sad. Reframing the situation also suggested some new possible solutions to try.]

We called up the teacher at her old school. The teacher talked to Sarah and told her the whole school was proud of her. The staff at the other school wanted her to succeed in this new school with the new challenges. We made a point of calling her mother at work during her break once a week, and when her mother went on vacation, she sent letters to Sarah. Also, I set aside fifteen to thirty minutes one day a week to talk with Sarah about the problem.

The results have been amazing. The times of crying gradu-

ally lessened. I could see it. This past week we did not even have
a tear. She seems happy and eager to help.
Now I can go to work on the other three students.

Discussion. It is hard to stop using solutions that have
worked in the past, even though they are not helping in the current
problem situation. Reframing, because it changes one's view of the
problem situation, generates new alternative solutions to be used in
what have become chronic problem situations.

If at this point you are still somewhat reluctant to try
reframing, you might be encouraged to do so by the experience of
the teacher in our final case example in this chapter. This teacher
combined reframing with other techniques (described later) to solve
interrelated problems among three of her students. We have
included this case example because it illustrates the positive effect
using ecosystemic techniques has on the person using them.

*Case Example: Pouter, Antagonist, and Tattletale or Unique
Problem Solver, Concerned Classmate, and True Friend?*

Sheryl, Peggy, and Gail often could not get along. Their behavior
in the classroom was disruptive. Sheryl would pout and answer
questions by forming words with her lips but not making any
sounds. She acted shy or coy. She was often off task, did not listen
during instruction, and failed to complete most assignments. Peggy
yelled at Sheryl in the middle of class. Peggy also pouted and
refused to sit next to Sheryl when it was necessary for a classroom
activity. Gail often tattled on Peggy for a variety of alleged
misdemeanors.

I had tried a number of approaches with these three in the
past. With Sheryl, I had ignored her pouting. I had humored her
and given her extra attention. I had tried to reason with her. I had
told her she could pout if she liked but that I did not have time to
wait for her response, so when she was ready to talk to me, she
should let me know. With Peggy, I had tried scolding her for yelling
at Sheryl and for refusing to sit by her. I had also simply told her
to stop pouting and punished her according to a previously agreed-
on discipline plan. With Gail, I had tried to ignore her. I had told

her I did not want to hear about other people's business. I had asked her if what she was going to say was about her business. If she blurted out what she wanted to say about Peggy, I invariably did or said something to Peggy about it.

Now I will describe how I have changed my responses to these students and the results I have gotten.

Sheryl began the day pouting because she had no pencil. She pouted about forty-five minutes. She came up to me and began to "speak" soundlessly. I told her I could not hear her, so she sat down and pouted some more. I went to Sheryl's desk and reframed her behavior by telling her that it seemed as if she was having a bad day and that her behavior was an understandable way of managing things. I said she might need to keep managing in this way for another fifteen minutes or even a half hour before she felt better.

Sheryl looked at me shyly. I went away. About five to ten minutes later, she came up to me and wanted help. I asked her if she was sure she was ready, explaining that if she was not, I wanted her to take the time she needed. The class laughed. I asked them why they were laughing. I told them I was serious. I said Sheryl had figured out a way of handling problems, and if it helped, I thought she should do it. They all stopped laughing. She asked for help again, and I helped her. The next day I reminded her to use her strategy for managing if necessary. She asked why. I told her that I thought it was her unique way of managing problems and if it helped, it was useful. There was no pouting that day. The third day there was a confrontation between us, because she was not paying attention when I was teaching. I reminded her that this might be a good situation in which to use her unique strategy, but she did not.

About two weeks later I commented to Sheryl that she had been doing her work and had not had any bad days. I also commented that it would be normal for her to have a bad day some time and when it happened she could just use her special way of managing things.

In working on the problem between Sheryl and Peggy, I decided to reframe Peggy's yelling behavior as concern for Sheryl's welfare and as a display of friendship. At first when I said this to Peggy, she looked at me as if I were crazy or did not understand at all. But she has not yelled at Sheryl or refused to sit next to her at any time since. Today Peggy pouted and refused to join her reading group, so I will reframe her pouting behavior as one of her ways of solving problems and encourage her to do it.

The next time Gail tattled on Peggy, I told her that I appreciated her concern for Peggy and commented that they must be good friends. I did and said nothing to Peggy about her behavior. Gail looked at me with a "foiled again" look on her face. Peggy smiled. To date Gail has not tattled on Peggy again. In general, the others in the class do not tattle on Peggy anymore, either.

There has been another result. Last year was my first year in a new school, in a new program, and at a new grade level. Previously, I had felt good about the job I was doing and enjoyed my students. This past year nothing was going as well as I expected. I was very unsatisfied with the quality of the work I was doing and felt very little rapport with my students. For me, perhaps the best result of these techniques has been that I feel more successful and am beginning to enjoy my job again.

Discussion. Using reframing will help you see many aspects of or truths about the behavior of others and allow you to select an aspect of or truth about another person that you would like to enhance or strengthen by behaving toward that person with this new description of her or him in mind.

In all of the case studies in this chapter, the teachers looked for something in their students that they wanted to see: best friends who could chat quietly and quickly and then go to work; a hardworking Sunday school student; or an awkward but cooperative adolescent. Looking for these qualities in their students helped the teachers and students create and find them.

Review of the Essentials of Reframing

Throughout the case studies, a number of points about reframing appear again and again. For example, reframing embodies the belief that problem behavior can be legitimately interpreted in a variety of ways, as well as the belief that everyone, even "problem people," views their behavior as appropriate to the situation as they perceive it.

In addition to embodying these beliefs, the technique of reframing involves a number of essential elements:

1. Awareness of your current interpretation of the problem behavior
2. Creation of positive alternative interpretations of the behavior
3. Selection of a plausible positive interpretation
4. Formulation of a sentence or two that describes the new positive interpretation
5. Action that reflects this new interpretation

Procedure for Developing a Reframing

This activity is designed to help you think through a general procedure for developing a reframing.

1. Think of a problem you are currently having. Imagine what happens in specific behavioral terms. What does the person do? When do they do it? Who else is involved? (Example: Bob comes in every morning and stands by Pete's desk. They talk and laugh for about ten minutes when they are supposed to be preparing their work for the day.)

2. How do you usually respond to the behavior, and what result do you get? (Example: I ask Bob to sit down. Usually I ask him nicely three times to sit down; then I order him to sit down. Then he usually goes to his seat, where he continues to talk or flash messages to Pete.)

3. What is your explanation of why the person behaves this way? (Example: He is irresponsible. He is trying to get my goat. He is stubborn. He is impolite. He does not want to follow rules.)

4. What positive alternative explanations might there be for this behavior? (Example: He likes his friend very much. It is important to him to reestablish contact with his friend first thing each morning. He is a very active boy who has found a way to ease into the classroom routine with a minimum of disruption.)

5. Based on one of your positive alternative explanations of the person's behavior, how might you respond differently than you have previously? What might you actually say or do based on one of these alternative explanations? (Example: "Bob, I can see that

your friendship with Pete is very important to you and that you like to take a few minutes each morning to check in with him. Sometimes having friends is more important than anything else.")

Now it is your turn. To try your hand at creating a reframing, turn to the practice activity on page 173. This activity will help you prepare to apply reframing in a problem situation of your own.

5

Looking for
Positive Motivations

The motive you attribute to the behavior of another person represents a hypothetical explanation for that person's behavior. Although you may regard it as true, it represents only one hypothetical explanation among many. Not surprisingly, the motives attributed to problem behavior are most often negative. For example, a child's repeated refusal to sit down when told to do so can be explained negatively as being motivated by a desire for power. If a student's behavior in a problem situation is thought to mean that the student is struggling for power that legitimately resides with his or her teacher, it is unlikely that an educator will be inclined to see a positive motive for what the student is doing. Nevertheless, attributing a positive motive to problem behaviors can help educators find more effective ways of responding to them.

The Positive-Connotation-of-Motive Technique

Identifying possible positive motivations for problem behavior is the essence of the technique of positive connotation of motive. In the last chapter, in our example of the student blurting out answers and the teacher steadfastly attempting to ignore the student's behavior, negative motives for the student's behavior are easy to find. For example, the student can be regarded as motivated by a desire to disrupt the class, to embarrass the teacher, to show off, or perhaps to control the lesson. If a teacher attributes any of these negative motives to the student's blurting-out behavior, then ignoring that behavior is a logical response. It holds out the possibility of minimizing the disruption, it does not suggest that the teacher is embarrassed, and it refuses to acknowledge the existence of a power struggle. All of these virtues are irrelevant, however, unless the problem situation changes. If the situation does not change, the teacher can formulate a new response based on one of the many possible negative interpretations of the motives for the student's behavior, or the teacher can try something different—the technique referred to as positive connotation of motive.

The first step in using this technique is to identify positive motives for the problem behavior. In the case of the student blurting out answers, a number of possible positive motives suggest themselves. For example, the student might be blurting out answers because he or she is genuinely interested in the subject matter and wants to demonstrate interest; likes the teacher and is worried that other students will not respond, which will embarrass the teacher; or be motivated by a desire to help the teacher ask more questions in the course of the lesson.

Attributions of positive motivation to problem behavior are just as hypothetical as negative attributions. However, since the truth about another person's motives can never be known, the value of attributing a positive motive to problem behavior is determined by its usefulness in changing the problem situation. If the teacher can accept as plausible that his or her student's motivation for blurting out answers may be enthusiasm for the subject instead of an attempt to disrupt the class, the teacher will find ways of responding to the behavior that are positive and sincere. The next time the student blurts out an answer, if instead of ignoring him or her, the teacher takes a moment to thank the student for such enthusiasm, the problem situation will be changed. Whether or not this change on the part of the teacher represents enough of a change to influence the student's blurting-out behavior, only time will tell.

Analysis of Case Examples

The following case examples help illustrate how attributing positive motivation to problem behavior transforms the problem situation and influences the problem behavior. The first case example illustrates clearly both how a school counselor attributed positive motivation to problem behavior and how a student responded to having his behavior described as being motivated by something positive. This case example is also interesting because it involved a school counselor working with all of the student's teachers. The school counselor formulated the positive-connotation statements with the teachers, but the teachers were the ones who actually said them to the student.

Case Example: The Thinker

Mike is a fifth-grade student who often refused to take part in classroom discussions or to complete written classroom assignments. He did not always refuse to participate in these activities. He seemed to do it on a selective basis. His selective refusals appeared to be based on his mood and willingness to participate instead of the content or difficulty of the work involved. [The hypothesis developed by the counselor and teachers attributes the student's behavior to his mood and willingness. As is generally true in problem situations, the student's motives are believed to be negative. A student refusing to participate in class activities because he is simply unwilling or not in the mood is not regarded positively.] Compared to other students in his class, Mike has average to above-average learning potential. On standardized achievement tests, he consistently scores at or above national grade-level norms and at or above the fiftieth national percentile rank. Mike's teachers felt that there was no valid reason for his not completing assignments or fully participating in classroom discussions, since he seemed to have the ability to do so. [The counselor and teachers have taken the facts and have interpreted them in a way that makes sense to them. This student is capable of doing the work, so his refusal must mean he is unwilling. The teachers act toward the student in ways consistent with their hypothesis about his motives.]

Mike's teachers have tried various techniques to get him back on track and become a more productive class member. His teachers have held discussions with him about the situation, explaining the importance of doing his assigned work on a more consistent basis and becoming more involved in classroom discussions. They have given him smaller assignments to complete, hoping that he would at least do some of the work. Parent-teacher conferences have been held. A daily assignment sheet of work completed or not completed was sent home with him every night for his parents to review, initial, and return to school. Special attention was given to him when he completed his work and demonstrated an interest in classroom discussions. Essentially, these techniques had little or no effect, except for some slight improvements that were made after a conference with Mike's parents. These improvements were short-lived, however, and Mike was back to his old refusal behavior after a couple of days. [The original hypothesis fit the facts of the situation, but the responses to the student based on this hypothesis do not seem to be helping. To use the sleuthing metaphor from Chapter Three, it is time to develop a new theory about the student's motives for the behavior, one that fits the facts but explains things differently.]

The techniques of reframing and positive connotation were explained to his teachers. Although the teachers were somewhat reluctant to try these new techniques, it was agreed that we would positively connote Mike's motive for refusing to participate in class to see if it might bring about more positive results. It was suggested that his teachers be consistent in what they say to Mike when he refused to participate in their classrooms. The basic statement that his teachers were to tell Mike was: "We know it is important for you to consider all the facts and do a lot of good thinking before you raise your hand and enter into the group discussion, so we want you to take all the time you feel is necessary before you raise your hand and are called on." For his classroom work, the positive connotation was: "We also feel it is okay with us that you do a lot of good thinking and consider all the facts before you start your written assignments in class. You need that time to get your thoughts together." [The behavior exhibited by the student was not talking during group discussions and not starting on his written work. When asked by the school counselor to attribute positive motives to this same behavior, the teachers were able to describe the student's not talking and not starting his work as motivated by the desire to "consider all the facts" and "do a lot of good thinking." The new hypothesis accounts for the facts (not talking and not starting his work) but explains them differently. These facts no longer mean unwillingness; rather, they signify thinking. With this new hypothesis about the student's motives, the teachers responded quite differently to his behavior. It is logical for a teacher to respond differently to a student who is "thinking" then to one who is "unwilling" to participate.]

Mike's teachers reported that he continued to refuse to do his work and enter discussions for the first two days after the statements were made to him. However, he also seemed to get the idea that that was okay with his teachers, because they did not nag him about getting his work done or about being an active member in a discussion group. [This is another important change in the teachers' behavior, and it is a significant change in the pattern of interaction between the student and his teachers.]

The teachers reported that, during the next few days, Mike would *act* as if he was thinking and considering all the facts but still did not complete his work totally or say much in classroom discussions. [The student appears to be trying out the new motive attributed to his behavior.] His teachers did feel that during this time he paid more attention to what was going on in class than he had previously. Four days after the statements had been made to him, Mike finally began to finish his written work and enter into group discussions more consistently. Now Mike's teachers report that he seldom refuses to do his work and seems much happier in the classroom setting.

Discussion. Since the attribution of motive to anyone's behavior represents a hypothesis, it is not possible to know if the motivations, either positive or negative, attributed to the student's behavior were accurate. It appeared to Mike's teachers that he took on the positive motives attributed to him. His teachers reported that at first he "acted as if" what they had said was true. In their eyes he seemed to be pretending to think and to consider things carefully. According to their report, it then became true, and he did think first and then participate. Perhaps, with their new hypothesis, the teachers created a positive self-fulfilling prophecy. They wanted to see Mike as a student who was thinking before participating, and in describing him as such, they helped him become it. Or perhaps Mike had always had a positive motive for his behavior, and the positive change was created by the teachers' willingness to develop a new hypothesis and to look for and find the positive motive that was there all along.

Positive connotation of motive can also be used when working with a problem that involves more than an individual student, as the following case example illustrates. This case example is unique in that the teacher had found an effective solution for controlling two students' behavior but was dissatisfied with what he had to do to maintain the control.

Case Example: Concerned Classmates

Richard and Matthew are students at the Learning Center. They attend a suburban school in an affluent area of the county and are on a time-release program for academic remediation at the center. Both are classified as learning disabled. Both come from wealthy families, with Richard's being "old" wealth and Matthew's being "new" wealth. (Matthew's mother is quick to point this out.) Richard is small for his age and not as bright as Matthew, but he is "quick" with his mouth and can verbally jab and subdue the taller, stronger, brighter Matthew. He has done this for a long time. Matthew, however, recently discovered his superior physical strength and would tell Richard to "shut up or I'll punch you" when Richard became too sarcastic or humiliating with his verbal putdowns.

At school, the boys were taught in the same room by one teacher. In the afternoon, at the Learning Center, they were quick to relate the events of the morning to the remediation specialist. They would tell all the "bad" things each had done, and there was a constant refutation of "facts"—who did what first and so on. This was quite time-consuming, and the positive emotional environment necessary for learning got seriously disturbed by the boys' tirades, putdowns, and telling on each other. Their game of one-upmanship was counterproductive.

If I was around, a quick look from me or a "knock it off, guys—that is enough" was sufficient. However, the control of their

behavior was external to them and based on my physical-psycho-
logical intimidation. If they could correct their behavior themselves,
I thought it would be a real improvement for all concerned.
[Although this teacher is successful in controlling the students'
behavior, he is not pleased with the method he is using, which he
describes as intimidation. He is willing to try something different
because he wants a better and, in his judgment, more humane way
of influencing the boys' behavior.]

I decided to positively connote their motive for "getting on"
one another. I told them how impressed I was with their concern
over each others' behavior. I said the fact that they had so much
concern for one another was very apparent to me, because each was
willing to sacrifice his own learning time at the center so the other
could get ahead. "Now, that is caring," I said, "to sacrifice your
learning time so that the other boy can learn." [This teacher was
able to identify a positive motive for the boys' behavior. He
described them as concerned and their behavior as motivated by a
desire to help each other learn and get ahead.] This worked well for
a week and a half (nine visits to the center). The teacher then told
me there was a relapse. The old behavior had started to reappear.
I smilingly approached the two boys and said, "I am not surprised
that you are still sacrificing your interests for each other. In fact, I
predicted it to your teacher. Old ways of showing concern such as
yours are not easily changed." [A relapse or reemergence of old
patterns of behavior is not unusual even after new behavior has been
initiated. Relapses are such a normal occurrence that a technique
called predicting a relapse (described in Chapter Ten), which helps
to maintain and even enhance the new behavior by defining
potential relapses as normal, has been developed.]

It has been two weeks since my comment to the boys about
their expressions of concern not being easily changed, and everything
seems to be fine. Positive connotation, plus describing the relapse in
their behavior as understandable, worked positively to help change
Richard's and Matthew's behaviors. External behavior controls
(coercion and intimidation) are no longer necessary.

Discussion. As this case example shows, the techniques in
this book can be used by educators in situations where they are

successful in influencing students' behavior but do not like the means they are using to accomplish the end. Responding to the boys' behavior using positive connotation instead of intimidation was a preferable alternative for this teacher.

Although most of the case examples in this book involve educators and students, problems can, of course, arise between colleagues. Since the techniques in this book apply to a wide variety of problem situations, we have included some case examples that involve co-workers to illustrate the point.

The next case example illustrates how using positive connotation to solve a chronic problem with a colleague can help enhance a professional relationship and work to the benefit of the students involved.

Case Example: The Conscientious Teacher

I am a school psychologist and multidisciplinary (M-team) manager. The M-team conducts Exceptional Education Needs (EEN) evaluations of referred students. One fourth-grade classroom teacher had a habit of submitting several referrals per year for M-team evaluations of children who obviously were not likely candidates for exceptional education programs. They were usually children who were below average in achievement and ability and comprised the "low group" in reading and/or math. They were usually less than one year delayed. Yet the teacher insisted that they might have a learning disability. These needless M-team evaluations created hours of work, mounds of paper, undue concern on the part of parents, and disruption in the child's schedule. At the end of M-team meetings, when the decision was reached that the child did not have a learning disability, the teacher would sigh and make disparaging remarks about how the poor child's needs would not be met because of technicalities. This was often confusing and disheartening to parents as well as frustrating for the other M-team members, who also felt that they had the child's best interests at heart. [This school psychologist has described a problem situation that touches a number of parts of the ecosystem. Not only school personnel and the student but also parents and home-school relations are involved.]

I had offered to consult with the teacher on cases before she referred them. I had explained that, if she wanted educational recommendations, a consultation with me or a non-EEN evaluation would serve as well as and be more efficient than an M-team staffing. But the teacher continued to submit EEN referrals indiscriminately, stating that she did not want to "overlook" a hidden learning disability and that she owed this to her children. [The teacher's comments about why she refers the children can be used as clues about how to proceed in this situation. She has stated that, from her perspective, her motive for referring the children is her concern for them. Her stated motive can be used as a clue in formulating the positive connotation.]

I decided to positively connote the teacher's motive for her inappropriate referrals. Although I did not like the result of her behavior, it was quite possible to imagine her motives as positive. [It is important to note the attitude the school psychologist adopted with regard to the teacher. She was willing to entertain the possibility that, although the teacher's behavior was undesirable to her, the teacher's motive for the behavior could be positive.] I hoped to accomplish two things. I wanted her to stop making the remarks she always made when the child was not recommended for an EEN program, and I wanted her to stop making inappropriate referrals.

Prior to an M-team meeting for a child she had referred inappropriately, I stopped in her classroom. I said to her, "You are such a conscientious teacher. I can tell by the number of referrals you make that you are really concerned about the individual needs of your children. Today you will be helping us to see that regular education teachers know how to teach below-average kids as well as special education teachers." [The school psychologist used the teacher's stated motive (that she owed it to her students not to overlook a hidden learning disability) as a clue in developing a statement to say to the teacher. The school psychologist then restated the motive in her own words and described the teacher as "conscientious" and "concerned about the individual needs" of the children, which was essentially what the teacher had previously said about her motive for referring children. The school psychologist then took the positive connotation one step further and complimented the teacher on her ability to teach these students.]

At the meeting, when the M-team decided that the child did not have a learning disability, the teacher did not act in her usual disgruntled way. Instead, she began to list several creative techniques that she could use in her classroom with the child. It remains to be seen if she will continue to refer children inappropriately.

Discussion. In the case example above, the school psychologist was able to establish a cooperative relationship between herself and the teacher with regard to one of her goals. It is too early to tell whether the other goal will be attained. However, changes that have already been made in this chronic problem situation increase the likelihood of further change. Given the teacher's initial positive response to having her motives described positively, one would expect further cooperation. It would be possible, but difficult, not to cooperate with someone who has described you as a conscientious, concerned, able teacher.

The school psychologist altered her perspective on the situation, and both the teacher and the school psychologist subsequently altered their behavior. The school psychologist was able to see a positive motive for the teacher's referrals and based her response to the teacher on this perspective. The teacher, on hearing not only her motive but also her ability as a teacher so clearly recognized, changed her perspective and her behavior during the M-team meeting.

In addition to showing how positive connotation can be applied, the next case example is helpful because it reveals the struggles that a teacher may experience in applying the ideas in this book.

Through the dialogues she includes, the teacher shows how easy it is to slip into an unhelpful pattern of interaction. She also shows how scary it can be to initiate a different way of responding to problem behavior and how difficult it can be to maintain this new, different way of reacting if the student initially continues to respond in the old way.

Case Example: Working Hard in Absentia

Abigail did not appear for school until well into the third week of September. Shortly after her arrival, I examined her cumulative school record and discovered a pattern of chronic absenteeism beginning in the third grade. She was absent an average of two to five days per week. In addition, she was tardy as often as two or three times a week. A closer investigation of her record did not reveal any suggestion of school phobia. The majority of absentee dates were carefully documented with excuses signed by one or both parents. Also, there was no record of any illness serious enough to warrant such a high degree of absenteeism.

Early in the school year, I attempted to discuss the problem with Abigail in a private conference. She was very defensive, claiming that she only missed school when she was ill. However, in the weeks that followed, I could not detect any signs of illness, not even mild cold symptoms, following her absences.

Prior to learning about reframing and positive connotation, I had consciously or unconsciously begun dealing with the problem by "negative connotation." One example of my attempt to solve the problem is contained in the following dialogue, as closely as I can remember it, between Abigail and me:

ME: Abigail, you must go to school. Attending school is just like holding a job. Failure to get to school indicates a lack of responsibility on your part.

ABIGAIL: Ain't you a trip. I am sick. I can't come to school when I'm sick. I'm not going to infect the whole school with my flu and cold symptoms. Call my mother and she'll tell you how sick I really am. Quit bugging me. It's none of your business whether or not I come to school.

ME: (now beginning to become somewhat impatient with her flippant response) You are a very lazy little girl, Abigail. You are not too sick to come to school. You just do not want to get up early enough to catch the bus. Look at how often you are tardy.

ABIGAIL: I am sick. This school makes me sick. It's like a prison, and we can't even go out of the building at lunch. You make me sick, too!

ME: (very irritated) Young lady, you are becoming

> very disrespectful. I think it is time for a little
> conference with the assistant principal. I will
> make out a disciplinary report immediately, and
> you can leave this room!

Abigail left, slamming the door loudly and almost breaking the glass. The result of this negative-connotation problem-solving technique was that Abigail did not return to school for the rest of the week.

Shortly thereafter, I learned how to use positive connotation in a problem situation. I decided to positively connote Abigail's motives for staying home. I tried this new approach with some trepidation, as the new method was slightly unorthodox for the extremely conservative climate of my school, but I was determined to give it a chance so as to improve Abigail's attendance. [We have found that it is often just this kind of commitment that makes educators willing to try something different.]

The following is another dialogue between myself and Abigail following her next absence, which lasted two days. In formulating the positive-connotation statements, I included some of the phrases Abigail uses in order better to communicate with her. [In Chapter Three we discussed how using a student's language can help solve problems.]

> ME: Why, Abigail, I am really surprised to see you in
> class. I am sure that whatever you were doing at
> home was very important, or you would have
> come to school. I think it is really cool that you
> are mature enough to recognize the importance of
> setting priorities. You probably stayed home so
> that you could work extra hard on your assign-
> ments so that you would get straight A's when you
> returned. Tell me, after you finished studying, did
> you get a chance to see any interesting segments
> of "General Hospital" or "Days of Our Lives"?

[The teacher has abandoned her use of what she termed "negative connotation" of the student's motives for staying home, that is, being lazy, irresponsible, and so on, and ascribes positive motives to her staying home, such as to work extra hard to improve her grades. Even when asking about watching television, the teacher assumes this was done after the student finished studying. The teacher does not know what the student did while absent or why she was absent. The teacher is trying out an alternative way of responding to the student. This new way of responding is based on the positive motives the teacher thinks could be possible.]

> ABIGAIL: *(her mouth falling wide open and her eyes bulging with disbelief, following a very nervous giggle)* Yeah, I sure did, and it was great. Sure beats school that is so dumb and boring—especially the teachers. I had a really great time and no homework either.

The class roared. Restraining myself because of my strong feelings about disrespect from students, I continued, hoping that some student would not report me to the principal for promoting truancy. But I was willing to try anything to get this kid to come to school.

> ME: Maybe you can give the other kids a report on what is happening on the soaps, okay?

[This teacher deserves a medal for the control it must have taken to maintain her new way of responding, given what had just happened. Her ability to do this is evidence not only of her commitment to change things but also of her willingness to look at the situation differently. Had she only been interested in manipulating the student, she might well have reverted to negative connotation and a disciplinary report at this point.]

I did not expect an instant miracle, so I was not too surprised when Abigail was absent the following Monday. On Tuesday, I spoke to her again.

> ME: Gee, Abigail, I see you took some time off to rest up after the weekend. What a trip! I bet by staying

> home and studying that you are much better
> prepared for your classes than any of the other
> kids.
>
> ABIGAIL: (*staring at me again in disbelief, but not quite so*
> *arrogant as she was in our last encounter*) Sure
> was a trip. I might stay home again tomorrow.

I restrained myself from shouting at her, "Oh, no, you won't!" and I dropped the subject.

I was really surprised when she made it through the rest of the week without an absence, but I never mentioned it to her. I just kept my fingers crossed. [Fortunately, the teacher is able to resist the temptation to praise the student. As you will see in later case examples, sometimes praising a student for a new behavior is followed by a return to the old behavior.]

I kept a very accurate record of her class attendance, the problem that I was attempting to conquer with positive connotation. The problem was not solved immediately. During February, she was absent two more times, but this was six days less than she was absent in January. During the first week of March, Abigail was absent one day. Believing the problem to be practically solved, I casually mentioned to her that I was really surprised because her attendance had been so good. She was not in school the following day. [Praise for behavior we like is a commonsense response that we seem compelled to make, even though it does not always reinforce behavior.] When she returned again, I positively connoted her motive for staying home, pointing out to her that I was sure she was staying home so that she could be better prepared for all of her classes on her return. She has not been absent or tardy since. This is the first time since September that she has attended school for three and a half weeks without missing one day.

Positively connoting this problem behavior worked well for both Abigail and me. Parent conference day was held on March 17. For the first time, Abigail's mother attended a conference without being summoned by the school. Her mother told me that she no longer has a problem getting Abigail to school. She cannot understand what happened to bring about this positive change in Abigail's attitude toward school. But I can.

Discussion. This case example illustrates a number of important points. It shows the concern an educator might have in using these techniques and having them misunderstood by colleagues or the administration. It also shows the commitment educators have to try something different if what they have been doing is not working. Also, it shows the teacher's determination to follow through with this new way of responding despite the student's initial negative responses.

Another point made by this case example is that even long-standing, chronic problems can be altered. This student had a long history of being absent an average of two to five days per week. At the teacher's last report, the student had attended school for three and a half weeks without being absent or tardy.

Finally, the positive impact that can take place on home school relations is clearly demonstrated. The student's mother no longer had to be summoned for school conferences and reported that she no longer had a problem getting her daughter to school.

Not all problems are as serious or long-standing as the chronic absenteeism discussed above. However, constant daily irritations can also make life miserable. In the next case example, the person applied positive connotation in just such a situation.

Case Example: Taking Time Out for a Co-Worker

Walter is a man with whom I teach. He used to pick on me constantly. Whether I was very busy or not doing anything, he had to make a snide comment about it. This went on every day. I wanted to go through one day without hearing Walter's comments.

There are many things I had tried in the past, and nothing seemed to work. I would tell him to mind his own business and get his own work done. Well, he would just laugh and keep making comments. I had tried to ignore him, and that did not work. I also had resorted to getting very angry and upset and yelling at him, but he would just look at me and make more comments.

I decided to try positive connotation to change the behavior. When Walter would start making his comments, I would look at him and with a very calm voice state that I was glad that he was so concerned with my well-being and that he was taking time out of his busy schedule to talk to me.

I was surprised at how well this worked. After I made the positive-connotation statements a few times, he stopped making the comments. He would just leave me alone. However, I noticed that after a few days of not making comments, he would start them again. I would look at him very calmly and again tell him that I was glad that he was so concerned. That seemed to stop him in his tracks. Now he is very nice to me, and when there is a problem, he even helps me.

Discussion. We can never know the real motive behind Walter's behavior. Perhaps he did mean to be "picking on her constantly," or perhaps this was his way of "showing concern." Without a doubt, he was "taking time out of his busy schedule to talk to her."

Regardless of Walter's original intention or motive for his behavior, for as long as this teacher could imagine only a negative motive, she disliked her colleague's behavior and responded in ways that contributed to continuing his behavior.

By positively connoting Walter's motive, this teacher may have changed Walter's motives for making comments to her; that is, he may have adopted the positive motive she attributed to him, which may have then altered his behavior. Or she may have, for the first time, finally recognized that his behavior did stem from positive motives. Perhaps all along he had only intended to be giving her some attention. If this was the case, her finally understanding and acknowledging this could also have contributed to a change in his behavior. Furthermore, if she came to recognize a potential positive motive for his behavior, she may have become much less irritated by the comments and may have no longer heard them as "snide" but instead as "interested."

Our final case example in this chapter illustrates how a teacher successfully used positive connotation of a student's motive and how an initial success can provide a solid foundation for a more productive student-teacher relationship. When the student in this case example had a relapse, rather than seeing this as a failure, the teacher acknowledged the student's prior success and elaborated on the original positive connotation.

Case Example: It Is Important to Be Exact

Clara is a thirteen-year-old student in an accelerated math class. Clara had no inhibitions. She would get up from her seat, stretch, and yawn loudly. She would talk to herself, disturbing the class and me, the teacher. Clara was extremely unorganized and constantly rearranging her folders and her books. Because of this behavior, she rarely knew exactly what to do and would ask for directions to be repeated, not once but many times.

Of all Clara's inappropriate behavior, the most annoying was her constant blurting out and asking for directions to be repeated. It became so annoying that at times the class would groan when Clara did this.

Invariably in response to Clara's outbursts I would demand, "Why didn't you listen?" or accuse, "You never listen!" Her constant answer was, "I was listening!" I also tried to ignore her hand waving or calling out and refused to repeat directions. This did not thwart Clara. She would ask another student or disturb others by looking around to see what they were doing.

I decided to try positively connoting Clara's motive for asking to have the directions repeated. I did not wish to sound sarcastic, so I determined to be very careful of my tone of voice. The next time Clara asked to have directions repeated, I replied, "I know that you listened, but I also realize that you just want to be very exact."

Clara was at a loss for words. She just looked at me and started her work. Twice after that she started to ask but stopped in midsentence.

For three weeks Clara went without interrupting or blurting out in class. Then, all of a sudden, she began blurting out in class again. This problem resurfaced after I thought I had successfully cured her of it. For three weeks she had not blurted out or disturbed the class in any way, and now it was starting again.

In the middle of class, Clara interrupted three times with questions about directions that had been given. After the third time,

I told her what she had done, expressing surprise that this had recurred after three weeks of "success." She claimed that she had only interrupted twice; however, I listed the three times, and she had to agree.

Interestingly, Clara was eager to overcome her annoying habit because, as she explained, she had not liked being called on because of her disruptions and had liked her three weeks of peace. Previously when she had been told to listen to directions, she had always objected. I had used the positive connotation "I know that you listened, but I also realize that you just want to be very exact." It had helped Clara to be aware of her actions, and the class was free of her disruptions.

Since there had been positive effects from the positive connotation, I decided to use the same strategy again. This time I told Clara, "I know that trying to be very exact can be frustrating, but I also realize that you are trying to work on your listening skills."

Since then, Clara has been very conscious of her behavior and has been very cooperative. So far she has again been successful in curbing her outbursts. We are both hopeful that her success will continue.

Discussion. In addition to illustrating the application of positive connotion of motive, this case example is also noteworthy because of the change in attitude on the part of both the student and the teacher. Positively connotating the student's motive seemed to help in the problem situation, and when there was a recurrence of the behavior, the student and the teacher were able to work cooperatively on the relapse. The teacher came to believe that the student really was trying to change her annoying habit, and the student acknowledged she had truly enjoyed her success.

Attributing a positive motive to behavior you do not like can help to improve the problem situation, because if you attribute a positive motive to the problem behavior, you may well be less bothered by it. Also, you may begin to respond differently if you think of the motives for the problem behavior as positive. Once these changes are made, the problem situation cannot remain the same.

Review of the Essentials of Positive Connotation of Motive

An attribution of motive, either positive or negative, to another person's behavior is a hypothesis. Attributing positive motives to a person whose behavior is problematic can positively change the problem situation. The attitude underlying positive connotation of motive is a willingness to be skeptical about what appears to be a negative motive and to believe in a possible positive motive for behavior you consider problematic.

In addition to this attitude, the technique of positive connotation of motive includes the following essential elements:

1. Awareness of the motives you currently attribute to the person exhibiting the problem behavior
2. Description of alternative motives for the problem behavior that are positive
3. Selection of a plausible positive motive
4. Formulation of a sentence or two that describes the new positive motivation for the behavior
5. Action that reflects recognition of the positive motive

Procedure for Developing a Positive Connotation of Motive

This activity is designed to help you think through a general procedure for positively connoting the motives for problem behavior.

1. Think of a problem you are currently having. Imagine what happens in specific behavioral terms. What does the person do, when do they do it, who else is involved, and so forth? (Example: Ron and Joe call each other names during class. When Ron, who is less bright, answers incorrectly, Joe makes fun of him. Ron reacts by calling out insults at Joe.)

2. How do you usually respond to the behavior, and what result do you get? (Example: I usually lecture the boys about their being old enough to know better than to call each other names, and I make comments about their being too mature to be so impolite. Often they then use this as ammunition and start calling each other immature.)

3. Why do you think the person does this? What do you think the person's motives are for this behavior? (Example: Both boys have low self-esteem and are trying to bolster their egos. They have no siblings, so they do not know how to get along. There are too many children in their families, and they are seeking attention. They are trying to disrupt the class. They are in a power struggle. They want to get each others' goats.)

4. What positive motives might there be for this behavior? (Example: This is their way of showing connectedness with one another. This is their way of expressing concern. They are letting each other know their limits. They are helping each other discover their own limits.)

5. Based on one or more of these positive motives for the behavior, how might you respond differently than you have in the past? What might you say to the boys? (Example: "Ron and Joe, it is surprising to see the concern you show for one another's work and success in school. One does not often see that degree of connectedness between students.")

Now it is your turn. To try your hand at positive connotation of motive, turn to the practice activity on page 174. This activity will help you prepare to apply the technique of positive connotation of motive in a problem situation of your own.

6

Seeing the
Positive Functions
of Problem Behaviors

Most of us are accustomed to thinking about the motives for and meaning of our own and other people's behavior. What motivates students and what their behavior means are familiar topics for educators. Our determination of the motive for and meaning of student behavior provides us with an explanation for the behavior. "She acts that way because she wants to control others" (motive) or "he comes late so often because he is forgetful" (meaning). The functions of a behavior (the nature of the relationships between a behavior and the other elements in the ecosystem) are often overlooked. They are equally important, however. A number of different ecosystemic functions for any behavior can be found if you look for them, although in problem situations it is often the negative functions of the problem behavior that are most readily recognized—for example, "when she combs her hair in class, it disrupts other students." Positive functions of the problem behavior, such as "when she combs her hair in class, it is a signal to me that seat work has lasted too long," are less easily identified. Nevertheless, these positive functions are worth looking for, because they very often hold the key to change.

In Chapters Four and Five we gave the example of a student who repeatedly blurted out answers because the student thought the teacher tended to ignore him or her. The teacher's response was to ignore the student in order to discourge him or her from blurting out answers. If the student had thought about the teacher's behavior in terms of its ecosystemic functions, one positive function the stu-

dent might have discovered was that the teacher's ignoring behavior
protected him or her from the punishments usually meted out for
blurting out answers. Had the student noticed this function, he or
she might have concluded that the teacher liked him or her and,
paradoxically, stopped blurting out answers. If the teacher had
thought about the student's behavior in terms of its ecosystemic
functions, one positive function the teacher might have discovered
was that the student's blurting-out behavior encouraged him or her
to rethink his or her methods of classroom questioning. Had the
teacher noticed this function, he or she might have concluded that
the student's blurting out answers had helped improve his or her
teaching and, paradoxically, stopped ignoring the student.

The Positive-Connotation-of-Function Technique

The technique of positive connotation of function involves
identifying positive functions for behavior previously considered to
have only negative functions and responding to the behavior in
terms of the positive function.

The blurting-out behavior of the student in our example
could serve any or all of the following possible functions in the
classroom: distracting other students (negative), disrupting the
teacher's presentation (negative), discouraging other students from
answering the teacher's questions (negative), helping other students
learn to accommodate distractions (positive), encouraging the
teacher to try a variety of different questioning techniques (positive), allowing other students more time to think and to reject possibly incorrect answers (positive).

When identifying positive functions for a problem behavior,
it helps to remember that a function is the relationship between a
behavior and the other elements in the ecosystem and is not the
same as an intended result. The functions of a problem behavior can
be very different from the result intended by the person whose
behavior is being described.

The technique of positive connotation of function requires
that you identify as many positive functions for a problem behavior
as possible and then select the positive function that, to you, seems
most plausible and that you can articulate with honesty.

The new perceptual frame acquired by identifying a positive function for the problem behavior will help you in determining how to behave differently in your particular problem situation. If the teacher in our example decides that one plausible positive function served by the student's blurting-out behavior is to encourage him or her to try a variety of questioning techniques, he or she may say something like this the next time the student blurts out an answer: "You know, all year you have called out answers without raising your hand and waiting to be called on. I have gotten angry, and I have tried to ignore you. However, your calling out answers has helped me to realize that I have been using the same style of questioning for a long time, and maybe I am due for a change. So I am going to try a lot of different ways of organizing my questioning. You will help me know which one is best, because when you call out answers less, I will know that my questioning is getting better. I think by working together in this way, we can make this a better class for everyone."

The key to the success of this technique is your ability to identify positive functions for a behavior whose negative aspects have been the center of your attention, to accept at least one of these positive functions as plausible, and to guide your behavior in accordance with the positive function you have identified.

Analysis of Case Examples

The teacher in the case example below had to do some determined sleuthing in order to find any ecosystemic function for the student's behavior, because the problem was that the student would do nothing in class.

Case Example: Inanimate Object or Enthusiastic Girl?

Greta, a child of average intellectual potential, behaved more like an inanimate object in my classroom than like a child. She did almost nothing. If she wrote two lines of work in two and a half hours, it was a good morning for her. She rarely participated in whole-group discussion and participated little more in small groups. When called on, she would hang her head and remain silent. She avoided interaction of any kind with both the teacher and her fellow students. She caused no trouble during class time; she would just sit and do nothing.

I had tried both positive and negative reinforcement techniques with Greta. She was positively reinforced for staying on task, for doing any work at all, and for participating in class. This had basically no effect. She also "earned" negative consequences such as staying in at recess to finish work and getting notes and calls home. Greta seemed to mind these negative consequences very little; she continued to do almost nothing in class.

I decided to examine the possible positive functions of Greta's behavior. [Here is a student who is doing almost nothing in class. The teacher's first task is to identify some positive ecosystemic functions of the student's doing nothing. It is easier to imagine how disruptive behavior might have an ecosystemic function, because it more clearly involves others directly. However, the absence of behavior, that is, not doing work, not interacting with students, presents a more difficult problem. How could the student's not doing something affect others in the classroom, and more particularly, how could this be described as having a positive function?]

I found that Greta's behavior of doing very little work had the function of saving me the time that I would otherwise have used correcting her papers. I used this time to plan and to help other students. [Having successfully identified some positive functions of the student's behavior, or in this case the lack thereof, the teacher now formulates a sentence or two to say to the student to acknowledge these newly identified positive functions.]

I told Greta that by giving up her share of my time, she was enabling me to spend more time helping other children and correcting their work and that it was rare for a child her age to make such a sacrifice for her classmates. I repeated this statement about the positive function of her behavior throughout the day as appropriate.

That day Greta spent most of her time giving me incredulous looks. As usual, she did no work. [Greta's surprised reaction suggests that the teacher identified a function of Greta's behavior of which Greta was unaware. This underscores the point that behavior can have many ecosystemic functions, some of which may not be recognized or intended by the person.]

The following day, the problem disappeared completely—along with Greta. She was absent for the next six consecutive school days. Needless to say, I wondered whether I had had anything to do with her absence.

On her return, Greta sat down as usual but got right to work. An assignment that previously would have taken her a few days to complete was finished in thirty minutes. She came to reading group with her assignment, participated actively in the group, and got a perfect score on the written assignment. When I marked her paper, I told her, "Good work." Greta returned to her seat and did nothing for the rest of the morning!

Since that day, I have guarded my natural tendency to positively reinforce Greta. When needed, I have repeated my original description of the positive function of her behavior with a slight alteration. I have also told Greta that I would be willing to correct her work, should she do some. Her work habits have shown some improvement, but what is most interesting is that she is participating more actively in class, answering questions correctly, relating to her peers in a positive way, and even taking a leadership position in small groups formed for discussion or for working on an assignment. Although she still does not complete all of her work, she is doing much more work than ever before and exhibits a more positive attitude in general.

The sullen, "inanimate object" has turned out to be a likable, even enthusiastic, girl named Greta.

Discussion. By looking at Greta's behavior in the larger context of the ecosystem of the classroom, the teacher was able to find a positive ecosystemic function for the problem behavior. Seeing Greta's behavior in this light allowed the teacher to respond to her differently. It also suggested to the student a function for her behavior that she may or may not have intended but that nevertheless defined her as contributing to the class and teacher through this behavior. Identifying this positive function of Greta's behavior and through this defining her as a class contributor helped create a class contributor.

This case example illustrates another important point. The teacher knew from previous experience that praise (which she called positive reinforcement) had failed to get the desired result. When she reverted to this natural, commonsense way of reacting to Greta, Greta immediately responded as she always had in the past—she did nothing. Fortunately, the teacher caught herself and was able to change her behavior.

Although the problem behavior described in the next case example is very different from the behavior described above, the school counselor, working with one of the student's teachers, finds a very similar positive ecosystemic function of the student's problem behavior.

Case Example: The Sacrificial Lamb

Brian is a seventh-grader who probably had the most negative attitude about almost everything of all the seventh-graders I have had to work with over the past fourteen years as a school counselor. He was very difficult to reason with or talk to. He was on in-school suspension for one month earlier this year for being involved with drugs at school. When he returned, his attitude seemed better, but it did not take long for him to revert to his old behavior. Everyone in the school, teachers, administrators, and counseling staff, had tried to help him.

In my initial dealings with Brian earlier in the year, I tried to discuss with him many of the things he had heard repeatedly over the past years: he was not working up to his ability, he did not get his work done, he was often absent or truant, and on and on. As hard as I tried to be positive with him and have him be positive, I was not being successful. [It is easy to imagine the difficulty, for both the counselor and the student, of finding something positive when the focus of their conversations was negative, that is, being truant, being tardy, not doing schoolwork, being involved with drugs, and so on. The objective facts in this situation leave little possibility of finding anything positive, it seems.]

I wanted to try positive connotation, but I was initially unsure what functions, especially positive ones, I could find for

Brian's behavior. I decided to work with our remedial teacher, Mrs. Weaver, who has four half-hour sessions with Brian each week.

The opportunity to positively connote a function of Brian's behavior arose when he decided he no longer wanted to get help from Mrs. Weaver. Rather than just give in and say he did not have to come to see her (it is voluntary), she brought Brian in to me, and we had a conference. We talked a long time. He was still being very negative. I finally said, "Brian, I am glad to see that you are willing to give up your time with Mrs. Weaver so some other student can take advantage of her time." [By looking at the ecosystem, including other students in the school, something larger than just Brian as an individual and his individual problem behavior, the counselor was able to find a positive ecosystemic function for Brian's refusal to work with the remedial teacher. Rather than focus on the negative aspects of the behavior, the counselor pointed out the positive function of Brian's behavior, that is, that it would give other students an opportunity to have extra time with the remedial teacher. Brian was willing to sacrifice his time for his schoolmates.]

His response was, "I don't care about other kids." [Fortunately, the counselor resists the temptation to convince Brian that he does "care about other kids." Whether Brian intends it or not, a positive function of his refusal to spend time with the remedial teacher will be that other students can have more time with her.]

After more discussion, I said, "Brian, as you know, working with Mrs. Weaver is entirely voluntary. It is your choice one way or the other. I am sure you want to think about this before you make your decision about continuing with her." At that point he said, "I know I don't want to be in the program," and he left my office. [The counselor has changed his way of responding to the student, but the student, at this point, is still reacting to the counselor based on their old pattern of interaction. We saw in the last case example how easy it is to revert to old patterns of behavior, even though they were not helpful. To the counselor's credit, he does not do this. He maintains his new definition of the problem situation and behaves consistently with it. He has identified a positive ecosystemic function for the student's decision to stop working with the remedial teacher, he does not attempt to convince the student of anything, and he only suggests that Brian take some time to think about his decision.]

The next day before classes started, Brian was at Mrs. Weaver's door asking if he could see her. He indicated that he indeed needed her help and asked if he could continue in the program. Since that day he has worked better for her and accomplished more than before.

As a result of my involvement with Brian and Mrs. Weaver, I feel my relationship with him is much more positive. Brian comes in on his own to see me and is beginning to be willing to talk with me.

Discussion. This case example shows how difficult, and seemingly impossible, it can be in a serious, long-standing problem situation to find anything positive to work with. The school counselor had tried for some time to find something positive to use in working with the student, and he reported that teachers and administrators had tried to help as well. In situations like this, where the behavior of an individual seems to have nothing to recommend it, it is often helpful to look at the functions of the behavior in the class or school. Even behavior regarded as very negative can have positive ecosystemic functions. Focusing on these positive functions of the problem behavior is a powerful way of promoting change in the problem situation.

A second point made clearly in this case example is how tenacious the patterns of interaction in problem situations are. This student has a long history of interacting with school personnel in a particular way. It has not been helpful, but it is familiar to him, and even when the school counselor begins to change the pattern, by changing the way he interacts with the student, the student initially maintains his old way of relating. Fortunately, the counselor is able to resist the temptation to take up the old, familiar way of interacting and maintains his new way of acting toward the student based on the positive function he has identified for the student's behavior.

Finally, the counselor's ability to continue to respond to the student in this new way reflects his having found a positive function that he believes for the problem behavior. By identifying a positive function for problem behavior that is truly recognized as positive for the class or school, the counselor could behave toward the student in a new way that was genuine.

Sometimes the intended result a student is seeking (laughter, in the next case example) is seen initially as having only a negative ecosystemic function. Looking at the function in a different light can lead to seeing a positive ecosystemic function of the behavior. Responding to the problem behavior with a view toward the positive function it may have for the classroom can lead to dramatic changes.

This case example is also interesting because the teacher involved two classroom aides in the intervention, as they were the ones having the difficulty with the student.

Case Example: A Serious Student in Comedian's Clothing

Brenda is a first-grade student who lacked self-control and was uncooperative when working with teacher aides. She had a kindergarten history of behavioral problems identified by her kindergarten teacher, but she had been exhibiting appropriate behavior under my first-grade teaching style. Unfortunately, her positive behaviors under my direction and structure did not carry over into situations where she was working with my teacher aides. The aides in my classroom work with the students in individual or small-group situations to reinforce skills I have taught.

Brenda's responses were usually silly and annoying when she was working with aides. For example, when asked to produce a rhyming word for "can," Brenda might say "like" and then laugh and look around at her peers, seeking their responses. Sometimes the other children would laugh, too. At other times they ignored her, because her response did not surprise them. Another example is when Brenda would answer a question with a loud "I don't know" and a laugh, when, in fact, she did know and could produce the answer when asked again. Another annoying behavior was Brenda's poking her hand at another student and asking or telling them something funny.

The teacher aides were frustrated by Brenda's uncooperative behavior. They were unable to carry out their responsibilities in the way that they would have liked. Also, it was distracting to me, because while I was instructing one group, I would be half attending to what Brenda was doing in her group with an aide. Sometimes when she was really disruptive, I would walk over and remove her from the group if the aide had not already done so.

In attempting to solve this problem in the past, the aides and I looked at Brenda's needs as we saw them expressed by her behavior. We decided she needed a lot of attention, so we tried to use positive reinforcement techniques such as (1) stickers on a card when Brenda's answers were appropriate, (2) verbal praise and letting her know the progress she was making, (3) personal comments to her before beginning to work with her, and (4) a note home when she worked well. At times negative reinforcement was used, and Brenda was removed from the group so that the group could stay on task. The aide would say, "Brenda, you are acting too silly, and we are unable to finish our work, so you will have to leave." She would then have to do the work alone at her desk without help.

These attempted solutions were only minimally successful. The problem was still there. It was an unusual situation, because when Brenda worked with me, her behavior was dramatically better than in the previous year, but she slipped into old patterns when working with the teacher aides. I wanted to see what impact positively connoting the function of her behavior might have when used by my teacher aides as well as myself.

In attempting to positively connote Brenda's behavior, I looked at both her motives and the functions of her behavior in the classroom. I thought the motive for her behavior was that she wanted to be funny and well liked by her peers. Although I had previously only seen the negative function of her silliness, which was disruptive, when I looked for a positive function of this behavior, I saw that it added humor and variety to the learning group. [The student had always intended that the result of her behavior would be laughter. Initially, the teacher and aides saw this having only a negative function. When looking for a positive function, the teacher was able to see this same intended result, laughter, as also having a positive function in the classroom. She was then able to use this positive function to suggest a new way for the aides to respond to the student's silliness.]

I talked to Brenda and said, "I have noticed that when you meet with the aides, you often act funny and give silly answers. I guess that is your way of giving fun to the other children and the aides. Am I right?" Brenda grinned very broadly and said, "Yes." I responded, "Well, that is what I said to both of the aides when they talked to me. They were concerned that you often do not know the correct answer, and they think maybe you cannot do the work. I told them I was sure you knew the answer, because you knew it during the lesson, but that you wanted to surprise everyone with a funny answer." I said, "You know, it's something that you would rather be funny than have the right answer! So, I have told our aides not to worry so much about your answers, because you are just trying to make things fun for everyone." I said very little more, and Brenda said nothing.

The next day, one of the aides met with Brenda and her group and commented before the activity, "Brenda, you really are a funny person." [A simple straightforward acknowledgment that the student is funny as opposed to an attempt to get her to stop being funny—this is an example of cooperation at work.] During the activity Brenda stayed on task and gave correct responses. A few times I saw her glance in my direction. The other aide made a similar comment when she had time with Brenda. She said, "You sure know how to give some of the funniest answers!" [Again, instead of attempting to change the behavior by asking or demanding that it stop, the aide cooperates with the student by simply acknowledging that she gives funny answers.] Once again, Brenda's behavior was appropriate, almost shy, and her answers were correct.

Since we began positively connoting the function of Brenda's behavior, each aide has worked with her about five times, and she has been quite serious about her work. The aides usually make a brief comment to her about being funny like "I wonder if this is a funny day." They are amazed at the improvement in her behavior, and they no longer have to wonder if she knows the material. One of the aides said she was going to try this approach in the lunchroom and see if it works with some kids there, too!

Discussion. In this case example the result the student intended to get (laughter) was initially seen as having only a negative ecosystemic function (disrupting the classroom). Rather than focus on just the function of the student's behavior, the teacher looked at the student's motive and the ecosystemic function of her behavior and found both a positive motive (wanting to be funny and well liked) and a positive function (giving everyone some fun) for the behavior. The teacher chose to combine the positive function and the positive motive in the statements she made to the student. When viewed from this new perspective, the result the student intended to get from her behavior (laughter) was seen as having a positive function for the learning group.

This case example is also interesting because it illustrates how responsive an individual's behavior is to the context in which it occurs. The student's behavior was different in different contexts. She behaved in one way in kindergarten with her kindergarten teacher. She behaved differently the next year with her first-grade teacher. And even in the same classroom, she behaved one way in the context that included the teacher and entirely differently in the context that involved the aides. This is an important point, because when problems arise, we tend to look inside the person for the cause of the problem and tend not to see the context in which the problem occurs or look for the aspects of the context that influence the problem. Had the teacher chosen to define this student's problem behavior as stemming from some internal deficit (for example, "she cannot attend to lessons because she has a poor self-image"), she would have been blinded to the aspects of the context that influenced the student's behavior. Keeping in mind that behavior occurs in a context, and that this context is made up in part of the interactions of the others in the context, is valuable in suggesting a place to begin to change problem situations. This teacher was fortunate that the situation showed so clearly that the same student, who obviously carried her internal state with her, behaved one way with the teacher and another way with the aides. The teacher's awareness of this allowed her to alter an aspect of the context in which the problem behavior occurred, that is, the ways the aides interacted with the student, and by altering the context, she influenced the student's behavior.

The teacher in the next case example does not even try to

guess the student's motive for his behavior. He just knows that one of the functions of the problem behavior is very annoying to him.

Case Example: Breaking Up the Routine

Roberto is a sixth-grader in my homeroom. A birth defect has slightly stunted his growth, and he is much smaller than anyone else in the class. What he does not have in size, he would make up for verbally. He was an incessant talker. He interrupted me very often, until I reached the point of sheer exasperation, daily. My only recourse seemed to be to focus on reprimands of various types, cold stares, "time-outs" in the hall, and similar negative responses. Roberto is very bright, and his outbursts were often correct answers or elaborations. Since he spent so much time talking, he often did not complete his work during class time.

Since reprimanding had not helped, I decided to use positive connotation and to focus on the function of Roberto's behavior in the classroom. I chose to look at the function of his behavior because I did not really know what his motive was for interrupting me so often. I did not know if he intended to annoy me so, but whether he intended to or not, he did. One definitely negative function of his behavior was to exasperate me. I could think of a lot of other negative functions as well. [It is not unusual in problem situations to be able to identify a number of negative functions of the problem behavior. Sometimes enlarging the scope of one's view, by taking into account others in the ecosystem, can help point the way to possible positive functions.]

In order to find some positive functions for Roberto's annoying behavior, I had first to observe and then to think about the circumstances in which he interrupted. I did this and then waited for my opportunity. One day in math class, Roberto began interrupting. I became quiet for a moment and then thanked Roberto for helping to make the classroom a more interesting place by breaking up the routine. I said it also gave me a chance to stop talking momentarily. [Although initially stymied, this teacher is able to find two positive functions for the student's behavior. He identifies a positive ecosystemic function for himself ("a chance to stop talking momentarily") and for the class as a whole ("breaking up the routine").]

When I used this intervention, Roberto was quite surprised and almost amused. During that period, I had to positively connote the function of his behavior several times. Roberto seemed to become more self-conscious, especially as he noticed how others would begin more carefully to scrutinize his behavior. During the next few days, I noticed a significant improvement in Roberto's behavior. He was making appropriate responses and attending to his work. Although he has not totally changed his behavior, it has improved dramatically. Also, our relationship has taken on an interesting new dimension. [It is not unusual to find that once a teacher uses these techniques in one situation, the change affects other interactions with the student.]

A few weeks after positively connoting the function of his interruptions, Roberto stayed after school to finish some work. He seemed upset, and I asked him what was wrong. He told me that he was sick and tired of being compared to his older sister and decided to get poor grades to show up his mother. As I considered what he had said, my first thought was, "How can I fix this? How can I let him know that he really could do just as well if he tried harder?" I decided instead to use the technique of symptom prescription. (This technique is described in Chapter Seven.) I told him that it was understandable that he felt frustrated. I commented about how difficult it must be to follow in the footsteps of his sister. I said that I thought it was all right for him to be satisfied with the work he could do and not what was expected of him by others. I told him that when I was his age I felt more comfortable doing just enough work to meet the standards and pass.

This discussion has had an interesting outcome, too. I find that Roberto seems to be taking more pride in his work. Another teacher who works with him came up to me the other day to tell me what improvements Roberto seemed to be making and was interested in knowing what had happened. It is hard to take credit for what seems to be so simple and straightforward a solution.

Discussion.   This case example illustrates well how difficult it can be initially to see the positive functions of annoying behavior. With some observation and thought, however, the teacher was able to identify a couple of positive functions of the behavior. The teacher's intervention also demonstrates how one initial change in the ecosystem (his positively connoting the student's interrupting) can positively influence later interactions (the discussion about the student's work and his then taking pride in it) and how this can transfer to other ecosystems (the student's improved work in another class).

"It is hard to take credit for what seems to be so simple and straightforward a solution," says the teacher in the case example above. The solution to a problem often seems simple and straightforward once we have found it. The difficulty is how and where to begin the search for the solution. The teacher had a difficult time at first seeing anything except negative aspects of the problem. Overcoming this perspective was the difficult part of solving the problem. Once he was able to entertain the possibility that there might be positive aspects to the problem and was willing to look for these, he had a place to begin. Having identified some specific positive functions instructed him how to behave to help create a solution. Having accomplished all this, of course the solution seemed simple and straightforward.

Sometimes the problems educators face are not with students but with their colleagues.

Case Example: An Important Role Model

The problem I had was with a fellow kindergarten teacher. As chairperson of the department, I felt under a lot of pressure to see that the curriculum was implemented, test scores were raised, the required amount of work was being done in each class, and so on. While I was under all this stress, one of my colleagues spent a lot of time with her students doing various "fun" activities such as singing and playing the piano for them. I felt like she was not "pulling her load" in the department. I also knew that I would have to change the way I felt if I wanted things to improve.

Since this was a departmental problem, I decided to look at the possible positive functions this behavior could have for me and the department. I thought about the added pressures of teaching kindergarten, the stress that I personally felt, and everything I was hearing about teacher burnout. With these ideas in mind, I figured out a possible positive function of her behavior. She was showing us a way to continue to enjoy teaching kindergarten and showing me a way to prevent burnout. I said something like the following to her: "I appreciate your ability to continue to enjoy your creative approach to teaching and not be hampered by the new pressures of teaching kindergarten." I commented that I thought it was wonderful that she could enjoy playing the piano as much as she did and not be forced to sacrifice her pleasure or the children's just because of the demands of the low test scores and workbook pages to finish. I said that with all the articles appearing about burnout and stress, she was an important role model for me and other teachers about how to continue to enjoy teaching kindergarten. The fact is, she was!

She was very receptive to my comments and said she was pleased that I felt she was creative. The following week our department was to be involved in testing all the children, one at a time. As chairperson, I was given the total responsibility for scheduling, distributing test forms, and handling all necessary correspondence. I was feeling really hassled but did not actively recruit anyone's assistance. Without any encouragement, my colleague ordered the additional tests needed, as she put it, "to make life easier for me."

Soon after, she introduced me to a friend of hers and went on at great length, praising me as being "a great friend and professional person" who always works so well with her. She mentioned that I always act supportive and share ideas with her. I had always thought of our relationship as neutral, but she described it in very positive terms. [Note how the changes in this case example amplify. The chairperson, who initiated things by changing her thinking and positively connoting her colleague's behavior, found herself affected by the changes set in motion when the kindergarten teacher took it on herself to order the necessary tests and praised the chairperson as being professional and cooperative.]

Over the past few weeks I have made supportive comments about her ability to be relaxed in spite of all the new pressures in early childhood education. I said that some people would not be able to continue with their tried-and-true ways of doing things with so much coming down from the administration about discarding old ways. I said she was a good reminder for all of us (the second positive function for me and the department) that stability is important and that there was merit in the old ways that kindergarten was taught.

For the first time in three years of my working with her, she was present for parent-teacher conferences and was prepared for them with art projects and other student work prominently displayed. [Note how the initial change has snowballed into these further changes in the department chair and her colleague.] I took the opportunity to comment on the large number of conferences she had and how wonderful she must have felt to be able to see all those parents. [Note the additional supportive comments and change on the chairperson's part.] Also, the art projects she displayed were the first ones she had worked on in almost a year. She says that art is not her forte, so this was a great change for her.

It seems the changes I have made in my thinking and in the way I talk to my colleague have had some impact on our working relationship. She is moving toward working with me more and working more on the prescribed curriculum. The pressure on me is easing.

Discussion.   As this case example shows, using these techniques in a specific problem situation with a colleague not only can help lead to a solution for that particular problem but also can improve the working relationship in general.

In all of the case studies in this chapter, an educator looked for some positive way a problem behavior was benefiting the larger group: a student sacrificing time with his remedial teacher, a colleague acting as a role model, a student providing a humorous outlet. Looking for the positive ecosystemic functions of problem behavior can help you to see the context in which problems occur and help you to use aspects of the context to formulate solutions.

Review of the Essentials of Positive Connotation of Function

Several points were made about the technique of positive connotation of function throughout the chapter. For example, problem behavior has more than one function, and some of the functions are positive. The function of a behavior can be seen in its influence on a single other person or in terms of its influence on the ecosystem in which it occurs. Finally, the functions of problem behavior are not necessarily the intended results, so there may be positive functions of problem behavior that are not initially recognized or intended.

In addition to these general points, the technique of positive connotation of function includes the following essential elements:

1. Awareness of the functions you presently recognize for the problem behavior
2. Identification of additional ecosystemic functions of the problem behavior that are positive
3. Selection of a plausible positive function
4. Formulation of a sentence or two that acknowledges this new positive function
5. Action that acknowledges and is consistent with this positive function

Procedure for Developing a Positive Connotation of Function

This activity is designed to help you think through a general procedure for positively connotating the function of problem behavior.

1. Think of a problem you are currently having. Imagine what happens in specific, behavioral terms. What does the person do, when do they do it, who else is involved, and so on? (Example: Greta, who has average ability, sits at her desk, hangs her head, and does virtually no work. She may write a line or two on rare occasions. When called on, she remains silent. She interacts very little with other students.)

2. How do you usually respond, and what result do you usually get? (Example: I have tried positive and negative reinforcement. I have praised her for any amount of work and any participation, no matter how minimal. I have kept her in at recess. I have told her the importance of doing her work. I have sent notes home. She continues to do almost nothing in class.)

3. What are some of the functions of this behavior that you presently see? (Example: She is slowing down the progress of the class. She is taking up teacher and student time. She is disrupting the class. She is preventing me from teaching in my accustomed style.)

4. What are some positive ecosystemic functions of this behavior? (Example: Because Greta is doing virtually no work, there is less work for me to correct, which saves me some time. This additional time can be used to plan and to help other students.)

5. Based on the positive ecosystemic functions suggested above, what might you say? (Example: "Greta, I had been upset with you, because it seemed to me you were wasting valuable teacher and class time, but as I thought about it further, I realized that when you do so little work, you actually save me time that I can devote to planning and helping other students. It is quite unusual for a student to sacrifice for her classmates the time and attention he or she deserves from the teacher.")

Now it is your turn. To try your hand at positive connotation of function, turn to the practice activity on page 175. This activity will help you prepare to apply the technique of positive connotation of function in a problem situation of your own.

7

Encouraging the
Problem Behavior
to Continue—Differently

Although all of the techniques in this book can be described as paradoxical, the technique of symptom prescription represents perhaps the most obvious challenge to common sense. In essence, symptom prescription involves asking for the problem behavior to continue, the proviso being that it continue for a different reason and/or at a different time and/or place and/or in some modified form.

In our example of a child blurting out answers and the teacher steadfastly ignoring the behavior, a number of symptom prescriptions are possible. (1) The teacher could ask the student to continue blurting out but at a different time. For example, the teacher might ask the student to concentrate on blurting out during the first minute of every lesson and during that minute direct questions at the student. (2) The teacher could ask the student to blurt out answers in a different place. For example, the teacher could establish a "blurt desk" in the room and ask the student to sit there when blurting out. (3) The teacher could ask the student to continue blurting out but in a different way. For example, the teacher could duplicate "blurt grams" and ask the student to first fill out the "blurt gram" and then blurt away with the contents.

The Symptom-Prescription Technique

The concept of cooperation is clearly revealed when symptom prescription is used. When you prescribe the symptom (ask the

102

person to do what he or she has been doing—differently), you implicitly acknowledge that the person has good reasons for behaving the way he or she does. You also tacitly communicate that life in school involves the negotiation of mutually acceptable behaviors. In order for you to use symptom prescription, you will have to think of the problem behavior in a different way than previously. A solution based on symptom prescription (as is true of all ecosystemic techniques) can represent a change in your interpretation of the problem behavior, an acceptable change in the problem behavior, or both.

Analysis of Case Examples

The following case example illustrates how a teacher used symptom prescription to alter how and when the student performed the problem behavior. The strategy this teacher developed with the student's mother combined reframing and symptom prescription.

Case Example: The Classroom Consultant

Chris is a ten-year-old fifth-grader who demanded constant attention. He would regularly come to my desk and make suggestions about how I should do my work. He would question most directions and assignments, asserting that his alternatives were better. He did not attend to directions and always asked to have them repeated. He procrastinated. He constantly sharpened pencils, shuffled papers, made frequent trips to the coat rack, crumpled papers, opened the window, and so on. When he would finally begin work, he would almost immediately complain or ask unnecessary, repetitious questions. If I took time to answer, he continued to find more to ask until I finally refused to answer. When I refused to answer and insisted that he get to work, he would sulk, mumble loudly, throw down his pencil, and proclaim, "I can't do this, and it's your fault. You won't tell me how to do it," and continue to make a scene. He interfered in interactions between other students and between the students and me. He would voice his opinion and attempt to impose solutions to problems that did not concern him. His behavior prevented him from accomplishing much and was affecting his achievement as well as disrupting the learning environment of the class.

My previous strategy was to deal with each outburst as it occurred. I had many patient counseling sessions with Chris, as well as parent conferences. I also assigned many detentions. All of these attempted solutions proved ineffective. Chris's mother (who had the same problems at home) and I developed the following strategy, which involved symptom prescription and reframing.

I told Chris that there were only a few weeks of school left, and I was concerned that the class would not have time to complete all the work that we had to do. To complete the work, everyone would have to concentrate and stay on task. I said, "You always have so many comments and suggestions, but I cannot stop teaching to give your ideas the attention I would like. So, for the rest of the year, you may ask any questions about your work immediately following directions when the rest of the class does. You may not speak out at all at any other time, but please write down all of your thoughts and comments. I will have a conference with you at the end of each day, when I can really give your ideas all the attention they deserve. I expect that you will forget and speak out quite often at first, because you have done it for so long. That's all right—it's to be expected. I will help you by reminding you with a glance—you know, by kind of lifting my eyebrows." [The teacher first reframed Chris's interruptions, complaints, and interference as "comments," "suggestions," and "ideas." She then asked for the student's comments and thoughts, but in a different way (written) and at a different time (the end of the day).]

It has only been a week since the plan was initiated. The first day, Chris threw himself into writing page after page of complaints and suggestions, all of which I treated seriously at the end of the day. He did very little else—but the rest of the class and I did great! However, the novelty wore off, and he began to lapse into his habitual outbursts. I laughed and said, "Aha, I guess this is one of the relapses I predicted." Chris's response to this comment was to quiet down. Further lapses were short-circuited when I gave him the raised-eyebrow treatment. He said, "I know, I know," and went back to work. He complained that writing took too much time, and he could not do his assignments. I told him that he had an excellent

memory and could stop the writing and just remember the important things. I agreed with him that his work came first.

[As discussed in Chapter Three, it is important to look for
changes in the problem behavior after initiating change. After using
the reframing and symptom prescription, the teacher noticed some
change in the student's behavior, that is, a decrease in complaints
and interruptions and an increase in work. As she noted these
changes, she modified the task associated with the symptom
prescription. She still had the student alter the original problem
behavior, but now, instead of writing it all out, he could just
remember the thoughts to be discussed at the conference at the end
of the day.]

A few days later, when we were to play a game outside, I
called Chris aside and said that, although we were having a kickball
game, I would end it early so that we could have our conference.
He said, "No way"—nothing too important had happened that day,
so we could just skip our conference. Hopefully, the strategy will
keep working for the remaining six weeks. By then I should be ready
for the eyebrow olympics.

Discussion.   The teacher in the case example above could
have just used the reframing of the student's behavior and have
thanked him for the time, effort, and energy it must have taken to
think of the number of "comments," "suggestions," and "ideas" he
contributed. Instead, the teacher decided to combine the reframing
with the technique of symptom prescription and ask the student to
share his comments, suggestions, and ideas in another way (written)
and at another time (the end of the day).

This modification in the pattern of the student-teacher
interaction produced enough change in the classroom to allow the
teacher and class to accomplish their work. As the student's
behavior continued to change, and he began to do his work and to
complain that writing out his suggestions took too much time, the
teacher modified the symptom prescription to fit the student's
changing behavior. What the teacher is attempting to accomplish
is to have a student who complains less and does more work. As
there is movement in this direction, she does not rigidly adhere to
the original task associated with the symptom prescription but

modifies it to fit with the improvement in the student's behavior and with the student's new view of the situation. It is the student who decides that writing out his concerns is taking too much time away from his work. The teacher simply cooperates with him by agreeing that his work comes first. This is a fairly common result of using the technique of symptom prescription. One of the characteristic experiences described by educators when they use symptom prescription is that they no longer feel like they are struggling with the student to get the student to change. Rather, they describe creating a new situation in which they can agree with the student about what should be done.

In the next case example, agreeing with the student about the problem behavior and the necessity of continuing it formed the basis of helping the student change her behavior.

Case Example: The Conscientious Calculator

Heather, who is very good in math, refused to do any computation in her head. She refused to do even the simplest problem or steps in the process, such as six multiplied by two in a multiplication problem, in her head. She insisted on breaking every problem into separate problems and writing them on scrap paper. Consequently, she was spending an exorbitant amount of time on her math at the expense of her other subjects. When I encouraged her to do the work in her head, Heather would get angry and say that she could not do that, had never been able to do that, and would never be able to do that. I tried putting a limit on the amount of time Heather could spend on math. This only resulted in her math being incomplete and her being angry. [Attempting to get the student to do the computations in her head and setting a time limit are examples of trying to change the problem behavior based on the teacher's view of the situation (which is that it is not necessary to write out all of the computations) without taking into account the student's view of the situation (which is that it is necessary). Such solutions lead the teacher to attempt to convince the student to see things the teacher's way in order to get the behavior to change.]

I decided to reframe Heather's writing every problem down as being a sure method of having all the problems correct. I decided to combine this reframing with symptom prescription. I told Heather that I understood that she was very concerned about having a perfect paper, and that perhaps she really did have to write everything down and should continue to do so.

[Instead of attempting to convince the student that she does not have to write everything down, the teacher agrees that perhaps she does. Given the fact that the teacher is now cooperating with the student's view of the problem and has reframed the behavior as a sure way of having the problems correct, it makes sense that she would encourage the student to continue to do it.]

I said that I had changed my mind because I, too, wanted her to have a perfect paper. Therefore, I thought it was best for her to continue to write every part of every problem down. I told her that in order to help her, I wanted her to get a notebook or use a section in her regular notebook where she could keep all her problems from every assignment. As a matter of fact, I told Heather she could show her math teacher her notebook, so that when she was not finished with her math assignment, the teacher would know that it certainly was not because she had not done a lot of work. Also, the teacher would know how concerned she was and to what extremes she had gone to have it all correct. Heather said, "Good, then she will know how hard I work."

[The teacher suggests not only writing down every part of every problem but also putting it in a special place, instead of on scrap paper, and keeping all of the computations. This represents two changes in how the problem behavior is performed, where the computations are kept and the fact that they are kept. The teacher further suggests showing the computations to the math teacher, which represents a third change. The reason given for doing and keeping the computations is to demonstrate how hard the student is working. Judging from Heather's reaction to this rationale, it fits her view of the situation.]

For the next three days, Heather wrote every segment of every problem in her notebook but kept "forgetting" to show her work to the math teacher. On the fourth day, I noticed she was not writing out every problem. When I questioned her, she said, "Takes too long." I said, "That's all right, if you are sure that you can do it in your head. However, you might need to write out some steps as you go along. In fact, I would really be surprised if you did not need to occasionally. So please be sure to write it down when you need to."

When I checked her notebook, I found that she had made only a few entries over the past two weeks. She is now doing most of her computing in her head.

Discussion. The teacher finds three ways in which she asks the student to continue the problem behavior differently. Essential to this process is the teacher's first cooperating with the student by agreeing with her that the behavior might be necessary.

The student's reaction, "Good, then she will know how hard I work," is typical of the kind of reaction people have when agreed with in chronic problem situations. The student has thought all along that it was necessary for her to do the computations in order for her math to be correct. She was not doing it for fun; it was a lot of work. Finally, instead of someone trying to convince her that she did not have to do this, it was acknowledged that maybe she did. Often with the technique of symptom prescription, the person whose behavior has been "prescribed" reacts by indicating that for the first time she or he feels understood. Interestingly, people often change when it is no longer necessary to convince others of the validity of their behavior in the problem situation.

Sometimes deciding which technique to use in cooperating with a student is determined by considerations outside the classroom. The teacher in the next case example had successfully used the technique of positive connotation of function with one of her students. However, with the student in this case example, she chose to use symptom prescription because of her concern about how the student's mother would react if she used positive connotation.

Case Example: Time to Work

Shannon is a student of above-average potential. He participated well in small-group discussions and had demonstrated the ability to master skills in all subject areas. Yet, when he had to work alone, he sat and literally did nothing. He did not talk or bother others; he just did nothing. A normal morning's work from Shannon was his name and the date on a piece of paper and nothing else. This behavior had been consistent since the first day of school.

Positive reinforcement techniques such as positive comments and "happy notes" for work done and for being on task had had no effect. Negative consequences such as having to stay in for recess to finish work had also had little effect in getting Shannon to complete his work. Interestingly, though, Shannon had been learning; he had gotten 100's on tests in math, reading, and spelling.

Involving the parent actually had had negative results. The mother was convinced that Shannon was retarded because he was born jaundiced. I had explained to her that this was unlikely and had tried to convince her of this by showing her test results to prove the contrary. She persisted in her beliefs, however, and insisted that I was unreasonable to expect him to work.

The mother's most recent negative response to the problem had been to ask me not to keep Shannon in at recess time anymore to do his work, because he had begun to act out at home. I complied with this, but I also expressed my reservations to the mother. The results of the new "outdoor policy" have been that Shannon went from 100's on his spelling tests to a 50 the first week and a 0 the second. He also failed a math test and began to get half or less correct in reading exercises.

Obviously, I needed to be careful what I tried with Shannon, since his mother was likely to hear about it and react negatively. Although positively connoting the function of his doing little work (it meant I had more time for other students' work) might have worked as it did with Greta (see "Inanimate Object or Enthusiastic Girl?" Chapter Six), it would probably have created some problems with Shannon's mother.

I decided to zero in on Shannon's quiet, possibly pensive nature during the work time. I told him that I could see that it was important for him to think and plan out his work and that that was a very grown-up thing to do. I told him that I believed it was important for him to be sure to think things through carefully before beginning to work, and that he should take at least five to ten minutes to think before he even picked up a pencil or opened a book during work time. Each time a work period began, I encouraged him to take all the time he needed to do that important thinking and planning and encouraged him not to dive into the work too quickly.

[The problem behavior the teacher is attempting to influence with symptom prescription is the student's sitting and doing nothing when he is supposed to be working alone. She first reframes his "doing nothing" as "thinking and planning" and then tells him to engage in this behavior for at least five to ten minues. The teacher changed her explanation for the behavior and then prescribed a definite duration for it. She underscored her prescription by encouraging him not to start working "too quickly."]

The first day, Shannon took his time and just sat there, as usual. There was little qualitative or quantitative change in his work.

The second day, he began to work about two minutes after sitting down. I reminded him to take the thinking time he needed. He did so for about three minutes, then began to do some work. He worked somewhat more than usual, on and off, all morning.

The third day, Shannon brought me a little gift, a package of cookies. This had never happened before. He sat down and took out his work. I reminded him to take all the time he needed to think and plan. He responded, using my language, by saying, "Today I think I need to work!"

And he did!

Discussion. The student adopted not only the teacher's language but also, apparently, her perspective with regard to his work. It is not unusual when using symptom prescription to see this kind of exchange of perspectives between the person using the technique and the other person involved. As the person using symptom prescription cooperates with, instead of struggles against, the problem person's perception and/or behavior, the problem person reciprocates. In this instance the teacher had been communicating in a variety of ways that she thought the student needed to start working. Once she stopped trying to convince him of this and instead encouraged him to wait and not to start working too quickly, he adopted her position and decided he needed to work.

In addition to problems involving students or colleagues, sometimes educators are confronted with problems involving parents. The kindergarten teacher in the next case example successfully used symptom prescription to solve a chronic problem with a parent.

Case Example: An Excellent Assistant

The mother of a child in my morning kindergarten class was presenting an ongoing problem for me. Mrs. West was coming into my classroom frequently during the class periods, interrupting me and the students to talk to me about her daughter's school situation. She disrupted the class activities quite a bit, especially since she spoke in a very loud tone. Furthermore, she did not observe the school's policies of arranging a prior appointment or of informing the principal of her presence in the school before coming to my room.

On one occasion, for example, I was teaching the class a calendar lesson. Mrs. West walked in (with her toddler in tow), walked right up to me, and stated in a loud voice that she had a question about her daughter's ability to identify the letters of the alphabet. Before I had a moment to answer, she continued to talk loudly and without a pause, until I attempted to stop her by stating that class was in session and a conference time would have to be scheduled. She ignored my comment and continued to talk until I walked her to the door and parted with her as professionally as possible. The students lost their focus on calendar work during this interruption and engaged in disorderly behavior. This type of incident occurred an average of once a week.

What I usually did to try to solve this problem was to point out to Mrs. West that I was busy at the moment and literally to walk her to the door. This diverted my attention from the students and resulted in their losing focus and being less on task. It did nothing to discourage Mrs. West from interrupting my teaching.

I resorted to having the principal remind Mrs. West of the school's policy against interrupting classes. He encouraged her to schedule an observation of the class by arranging this with me. She said she would do so but failed to comply.

I also tried scheduling both phone conferences and person-to-person conferences with her to discuss her concerns about her daughter. Since most of her questions required simple, common-sense answers, her child was not having any school problems that interfered with her learning, and Mrs. West's interruption of the class persisted, I became convinced that her priority was to be present in the class during the class period and that nothing would divert her from this behavior.

[This teacher has made a number of attempts to cooperate with this parent. She has been very willing to answer the parent's questions and has attempted in a variety of ways to modify the problem behavior. Since this has not changed the parent's behavior in a satisfactory way, the teacher continues to look for clues about how to cooperate effectively with the mother. She decides that she must figure out a way to cooperate with the mother that includes the mother in the classroom.]

I decided that I would have to change my thinking and behavior regarding this problem. I decided to tell Mrs. West that I could see she was very interested in her daughter and that she liked to come into our room during class time. I told her I felt complimented that the value she placed on my opinion led her to consult me about her daughter. I told her that it was fine with me if she would like to come into the class once a week. I said if she would get a sitter for the toddler, it would be all right with me for her to come in to volunteer her help in the class an hour a week on a day and at a time we would agree on. During her hour in the class, I would have her help the students with computer work, projects, and remedial work. I explained that she would have to use a soft tone of voice and give the other students time equal to the amount she gave her daughter in class. I said that due to her prior experience as a teacher (information uncovered by my doing a thorough study of the files), she would, no doubt, be a big help to me. I was sincere in these remarks. She indicated her pleasure at being invited to be my "assistant," as she put it.

She has complied with all of my requests. She has come in to volunteer her time from 9:00 to 10:00 A.M. the past two Wednesdays. All has gone well, so much so that I have been able to tell her frankly that it is a relief to me that she has stopped her unannounced visits to my class. I have also told her that she is a competent kindergarten "assistant" and that the children are being helped by her attention. My feelings have changed dramatically toward Mrs. West. I now feel we are working together instead of battling with each other.

Discussion. This case example shows well the adjustments and sleuthing that may be necessary to solve chronic problems. The teacher tried a number of ways of cooperating before she found the right fit in this problem situation. For example, the teacher tried to change the problem behavior by having the mother ask her questions at a different time (after class) or in a different way (over the phone). These efforts to cooperate did not change the problem behavior. They did, however, provide the teacher with information that suggested another way of prescribing the symptom: asking the mother to involve herself in the classroom—differently (as an assistant).

It is interesting to note that once the teacher figured out how to cooperate with the mother, while in the classroom the mother was willing to do everything the teacher asked. Nearly every aspect of the problem behavior was changed. The original problem behavior was no longer present, and the teacher transformed the problem situation into an advantage for her and the class.

In the next case example, the teacher used symptom prescription only as a last resort in working with a student. Once the student's behavior had improved, the teacher helped maintain the change by using the technique of predicting a relapse (this technique is described in Chapter Ten).

Case Example: Walking to Work

Helen was often off task during work time. She was out of her seat frequently. She would then wander aimlessly around the room and engage in conversation with other students. She would also leave the room several times to go to the bathroom and be gone for long periods of time. Consequently, she did not finish her work in school. I require that work not finished in school be taken home and completed. She did not finish her work at home and came to school with her work unfinished.

We have well-defined class rules and a set of consequences for breaking rules. Helen broke the rules often by the aforementioned behaviors, and I responded with warnings, exclusion, writing, and home contact. There was no improvement. I scolded her, tried to reason with her, sent notes home to her parents, and conferred with her parents over the phone and in person. I also tried moving her desk next to mine, but I rarely sit there, so I could not monitor her effectively. Anyone with unfinished work could not go outside to play during recess. Helen stayed in regularly. I even made her my prisoner by requiring that she stay next to me at all times and not allowing her to do anything without my permission. Even this brought only a temporary change.

Since Helen was wandering around aimlessly anyway and leaving the room frequently for long periods of time, I decided I had little to lose in attempting to use symptom prescription. All my efforts to get her to stop walking had not been successful, so I was willing to tell her to keep walking if it would help.

[When first using symptom prescription, some educators are concerned that they will make the situation worse. It can be difficult to imagine how asking a student to perform a problem behavior (albeit differently) will help. For this reason, many educators, like the teacher in this case example, initially use symptom prescription only when they feel there is nothing to lose. This is not surprising. Until one has experienced the noncommonsense and sometimes dramatic results of cooperating with someone in a problem situation, it makes sense to be skeptical.]

I said to Helen that I realized she needed to get up and walk around the room sometimes. I told her she should walk around until she was ready to sit down and do her work.

[This symptom prescription is simple and straightforward. The child is walking around anyway. The teacher tells her to go ahead and walk and sit down when ready to do her work. She cooperates with Helen by expressing her awareness of Helen's need to walk sometimes. The change in the problem situation can be understood with the new explanation of the reason the student walks around. Instead of wandering aimlessly, Helen is now walking with purpose; she is someone who needs to walk in preparation to work. The teacher also subtly adds an ending point;

that is, the student is told to walk around until ready to sit down and do her work.]

Helen's jaw dropped. She sat down within minutes of my saying she should walk until ready to do her work. She was in no trouble the rest of the week. To be fair, I must add that two of these days we were on field trips and she did not usually have behavior problems on a trip.

I have Helen again for summer school. Since it started, she has been sitting and working. I predicted a relapse to her and told her it would be normal if she were to start walking again. I also said that if she felt it was necessary, she should walk around a bit before starting her work. She came into the classroom and sat down. When I saw her out of her seat, I told her that I understood it was "walking time." She immediately sat down. Once, while she was sitting down, I suggested to her that she get up and walk if she needed to. She walked around her desk once and sat down.

[This teacher seems to have overcome her fear of using symptom prescription. She is even suggesting to the student, while the student is sitting, that she might need to get up and walk. Although this may not seem to make sense initially; from a cooperative perspective, it does. If walking around for a while first helps the student settle down and work, it makes sense for a teacher to encourage this behavior.]

Not only has she been sitting down, but up until this past week, her work has been done regularly. For the last two days she has not completed the majority of her work; however, she has still been sitting down. I think I will try reframing with the unfinished work problem. Symptom prescription worked well. Now I am ready to try another technique.

Discussion. Although some educators use the ideas in this book early on in problem situations, some, like this teacher, prefer to try other strategies first. With symptom prescription in particular there is at first the concern that asking someone to perform a problem behavior will make things worse. Sometimes ecosystemic techniques produce an initial increase in the behavior, as the teacher experienced in the case example "Distant Drums" in Chapter Three. However, any change—even a temporary increase in the problem behavior—is a change in the pattern of the chronic problem situation that can provide clues leading to alternative solutions.

The school psychologist in the next case example devised a plan for solving the problem based on the student's view of the situation and what he specifically did and did not want to do. The psychologist cooperated so well with the student that he eventually had to convince the school psychologist that he should stop the behavior he had advocated.

Case Example: The Privilege of Homework

Cavan is a sixth-grade student with a history of difficulties with homework completion. He had generally wasted time in school and refused to do schoolwork at home. Recently, his teacher asked for a consultation with me, the school psychologist, because Cavan had started a habit of chronic lying to both his parents and his teachers regarding his homework. When his parents told him to do his homework, he would say he did not have any. When his teacher asked him why he had not done his homework, he would say he had not had time because his parents made him do chores or go shopping or something of that sort. Cavan's parents and teachers responded to the lies with further probing, nagging, and punishment, which seemed to make Cavan very anxious and caused his lying to escalate. Apparently a vicious cycle of interactions had been established.

In the past, an assignment notebook system had been used, but it was unsuccessful because Cavan continuously "forgot" it or forged his parents' signatures on it. Cavan's teacher had weekly telephone contacts with his parents, but these were considered unproductive, because both the parents and the teachers were frustrated and very emotionally involved. Cavan seemed to be the only person who was uninvolved. His only involvement consisted of keeping the cycle going by doing nothing. He repeatedly stated that he did not like to do schoolwork at home.

I decided to use symptom prescription, and then reframing, to help Cavan reconceptualize the concept of homework. His teacher and parents agreed to the following plan: (1) I told Cavan that it was understandable that he did not like doing schoolwork at home. After all, schoolwork was *school*work, and why should it be done at home? (2) The assignment notebook system was abandoned. (3) The last hour of every school day was Cavan's study period. It was agreed that Cavan would do his assignments during that period and stay at school each day until all of his work was completed. Cavan was not to be allowed to take work home—after all, it was schoolwork, not homework.

The plan worked well for the first six days. Cavan completed all work in school, but usually he had to stay after school up to one-half hour in order to complete it. On the seventh day, Cavan was in a hurry to get home, because the weather was nice and he wanted to play soccer with his friends. He asked for permission to take a short assignment home to complete it. His teacher, as I had instructed her, stated, "Schoolwork is for school, not home," and insisted that he finish it at school. The next day (Thursday) Cavan was absent. When he returned on Friday, he asked if he could make up his missing assignments at home over the weekend. The teacher stated, "Schoolwork is for school, not home." Cavan became angry and asked to see me, as I was the one who had set up this plan. When I saw him, he complained bitterly about how stupid the plan was—how he was having to spend more time at school, and why could he not take work home like everyone else did? I replied that maybe he deserved the privilege of doing his work at home and that I would check with his teacher and parents to see if they agreed. Cavan was subsequently allowed to take his work home. Seven school days have since elapsed, and Cavan has consistently completed his work, doing most of it in school and the remainder at home.

Discussion. This case example reminds one of the saying "Be careful what you ask for—you might just get it." Fortunately for the student, the school psychologist continued to cooperate with him, and as the student's behavior and perspective of the situation changed, the psychologist modified the symptom prescription to fit with the changes.

This case example also shows how drastically the perspectives can alter in a problem situation, and then how dramatically the problem can change. The student's behavior had deteriorated to the point that he was chronically lying, and the parents and teacher were so frustrated that they were no longer able to work together effectively. The school psychologist's ability to cooperate with the student and propose an entirely different way of interpreting the problem not only helped the teacher and parents begin working together again but also had the student insisting he be allowed to do what they had wanted him to do all along. It is important to remember that even if Cavan had not insisted on having the "privilege" of taking schoolwork home, the problem would have been solved.

In all of the case examples in this chapter, the educator involved looked for a way to use problem behavior positively. He or she stopped attempting to convince the problem person that the problematic behavior should be abandoned. Instead, the behavior was accepted as somehow useful in the situation, and for this reason it was encouraged to continue in some modified way. Cooperating in this way led to an exchange of perspectives between the people involved, so that a kindergarten mother who insisted on being present in the classroom was obliged and returned the favor by being an excellent assistant. A student who did not start his work when encouraged by his teacher not to start it too soon retorted that he thought it was time he got to work. A student who laboriously computed all her math, when given a special place and recognition for doing so, stopped this behavior. Even walking around the room and refusing to do schoolwork at home ceased once the behavior was accepted as understandable.

Review of the Essentials of
Symptom Prescription

Symptom prescription is perhaps the most obviously paradoxical of the techniques described in this book. It requires adopting the attitude that the problem behavior itself may be useful in the situation and/or that the person engaging in the behavior has a good reason for the behavior under the circumstances.

With this view in mind, the technique of symptom prescription involves the following essentials:

1. Awareness of your current attempts to convince the person to stop the problem behavior
2. Identification of ways the problem behavior can be performed differently
3. Selection of one or more of the different ways that the behavior can be performed and positively regarded in some way
4. A request that the behavior be continued in one of these modified positive ways

Procedure for Developing a Symptom Prescription

This activity is designed to help you think through a general procedure for using the technique of symptom prescription.

1. Think of a problem you are currently having. Imagine what happens in specific behavioral terms. Who is involved? What happens? Who does or says what to whom? (Example: Chris demands lots of attention. He comes to my desk and makes suggestions about how I should work. When I give directions, he makes alternative suggestions and insists they are better. At other times, he does not listen and asks that directions be repeated. He does not get down to work when an assignment is given and instead sharpens pencils, shuffles paper, and so on. Shortly after beginning the assignment, he will ask for more repetitious unnecessary directions. He also involves himself in nearly every interaction between other students in the classroom and between me and students. His behavior is disruptive and prevents him from getting his work done.)

2. How do you usually respond to get the person to stop the behavior? What result do you usually get? (Example: If I answer his questions, he asks more. If I refuse to answer, he throws down his pencil and complains loudly and bitterly that he cannot do the work and that it is my fault because I will not tell him how. When he interferes with me and the other students, I tell him politely at first and then rather rudely that it is none of his business. This has no effect at all. He remains convinced, apparently, that it is his business.)

3. What are some ways the problem behavior could be performed differently? (Example: He might write down the

suggestions to be shared at the end of the day in a conference with me. He might be asked to make an announcement to the class just prior to my giving instructions that it is time to pay careful attention.)

4. How might you request that the person perform the modified behavior in a positive way? What might you actually say? (Example: "Chris, you always have so many comments and suggestions about things throughout the day, but I cannot stop teaching to give your ideas the attention you would like. I would like you to write down all of your thoughts and comments, and, at the end of each day, when I can give your ideas the attention they deserve, we will have a conference.")

Now it is your turn. To try your hand at symptom prescription, turn to the practice activity on page 176. This activity will help you prepare to apply symptom prescription in a problem situation of your own.

8

Influencing the
Problem Indirectly

All of the techniques explained thus far in Part Two have focused on changing some aspect of the problem behavior directly. The techniques discussed in Chapters Eight and Nine promote change in problem situations indirectly. The idea is that since all elements in an ecosystem are related, a change in a nonproblem part of the ecosystem has the potential to influence the problem behavior.

In this chapter we discuss how focusing on a nonproblem aspect of the problem situation or a nonproblem part of the larger classroom ecosystem can influence problem behavior. This can be illustrated by referring to our example of the student who blurts out answers and the teacher who is determined to ignore the blurting out in order to discourage it. Although their respective behaviors are not producing happy results, the relationship between the teacher's behavior and the student's behavior is symmetrical; that is, each behavior encourages the other. Sometimes continuing to focus on the problem in situations like this gives the problem ever more significance without producing a solution. The problem becomes like a speck on a clean window. Although there is a wide world outside the window, if you look at it too closely, all you will see is the speck of dirt.

If the teacher in the blurting-out example were to attempt indirectly to influence the problem behavior, he or she would look for ways to do something different in his or her nonproblem contacts with the student. For example, if in the lunchroom the student is eating a snack the teacher also likes, the teacher might mention it; if the student is wearing an attractive article of clothing, the teacher might comment on it; or if the student has a hobby that the teacher finds interesting, the teacher might express that interest. The key is that whatever the behavior of the teacher, it is new or different and is not connected to the problem behavior. This new behavior may occur in a situation other than the problem situation or in the problem context.

The Storming-the-Back-Door Technique

Storming the back door is our metaphorical way of saying that in problem situations the problem is like a strongly bolted door standing between you and a more constructive relationship. At times you may find a battering ram strong enough to break down the door, but the result always involves a fair amount of destruction. However, it is sometimes possible to walk around to the frequently unlocked back door and just walk in.

Every other technique we describe represents the adaptation of a strategy used in a therapeutic setting to promote change. We and our students came up with storming the back door when we were forced to look for ways to apply ecosystemic ideas in the face of behaviors that did not respond to any of the problem-focused ecosystemic techniques we had tried.

Since storming the back door involves only nonproblem behaviors, characteristics, or aspects of a person or his or her relationships, many people find it easier to use initially than a problem-focused technique such as positive connotation of motive. The reason is straightforward. It is easier to comment positively about something when it initially presents itself as positive or at least neutral. Finding something genuinely positive to think or say about a problem is more difficult. Although this technique was initially developed after we found that nothing else seemed to be working with a problem behavior, it is often the first choice for people once they learn it.

Analysis of Case Examples

In each of the case examples in this chapter, the teachers involved made positive comments to students with whom they had a problem. These comments were not about the problem behavior, yet they seemed to influence it. Some people might explain this by suggesting that students involved simply began to like their teachers more as a result of the teacher's positive comments. We think it demonstrates how ecosystems function.

In the first case example, the teacher is struggling valiantly to solve one of those little problems that can occasionally make life in schools so frustrating.

Case Example: Whose Is This?

The problem was that Josephine, a very capable student in an accelerated reading group, was not following directions to head her paper with her full name and the date. She did this on a regular basis, and I found it most annoying.

The problem occurred during my first-hour sixth-grade reading class. Josephine would complete her assignment neatly and accurately but refuse to "head" her paper. I expect this occasionally from all students; however, Josephine did it on a regular basis. I had placed a sample heading on the bulletin board as a reminder. Josephine ignored it.

Initially, my response to an unheaded paper had been, "Whose paper is this?" Response: "Oh, that's Josephine's!" On collecting a paper from her desk, I would say, "Josephine, I will need your name and the date on this," which resulted in a snippy, sassy response and a hastily scribbled heading. As the weeks progressed, this continued to be a problem with Josephine. Needless to say, it became a growing irritant.

Besides the above-mentioned attempts to solve the problem, I tried reminding Josephine to head her paper at the beginning of the written activity; this usually got me a first name only and no date. I threatened to throw out unheaded papers and have them redone, which was an empty threat made in anger, because I do not believe in doing this. I tried reminding the entire class to head their papers before they start; this worked with Josephine in perhaps one out of ten papers. I had seriously considered having the girl come in after school and head perhaps fifty or sixty papers for practice;

I chose against this, not wanting to deal with her resulting "attitude" that would surely follow.

I had become more and more irritated by Josephine and her increasing "snippy" attitude. [Clearly the problem in this case example represents no crisis. Nevertheless, a thoughtful, reflective teacher is spending a considerable amount of time trying to figure out what to do and becoming more annoyed with each failure. Having tried everything he knows how to do and is willing to do, the teacher seems to be feeling powerless.] With nothing to lose, I decided to try storming the back door with Josephine and her unheaded papers. I decided to capitalize on Josephine's pride in her personal appearance, something that is far more important to her right now than schoolwork and following directions.

Josephine arrived early to class on Tuesday, and I proceeded with my plan. "And who is *this* in a new purple outfit? That color looks good on you, Jo." "Thanks," she replied (nothing more). I proceeded with class, assigned a brief follow-up exercise, and collected the papers (and held my breath). Sure enough, she turned in a perfect paper with a neat heading. Can't be, I thought. Next day, I tried this: "New moccasins, Jo? Real neat; they're you!" Again, without any reminder, Josephine headed her paper. I began to "welcome" her appearance in class more every day, sometimes just saying, "Hi, Jo! And how's it going this morning?"

About eight days passed smoothly, with the usual morning greetings. Then, one morning before class began, I was preoccupied with several other students right up to the bell, and I failed to acknowledge Jo's presence. When I collected the papers (you guessed it), there was no name on Josephine's. Considering we had come so far, I was unwilling to revert to our old pattern. So I said, "Josephine, your name, please. You know, Jo, I often forget to put my name on things when I have something else on my mind." Her pleasant response was, "How silly of me; I just wasn't thinking. Sorry!" A few days followed, with her papers headed as usual. Then, I received another one with just Josephine written on it. I said, "Josephine, I know it is hard to remember; we often have so much to remember." She responded, "Thanks, Mr. Coburn; I'll do it right now." [Here the teacher passed up a perfect opportunity to fall back into the old pattern of interaction with Josephine! Storming the back door had produced enough change in the problem situation so that when the problem behavior reappeared, the teacher found a way to change his response to it. The result seems to be that the problem behavior remained an exception instead of once again becoming the rule.]

Since then, I have kept simple records of the responses to these techniques, and I must say that they work, and I really feel good about it. The girl does not always need a compliment now; sometimes a nod or a wink is enough. Our rapport has improved 90 percent. Although she is not in my social studies class, she chose to bring in some Spanish menus from her aunt to share with me before reading class. (I was pleased and I asked if I could use them for the day with my classes; her face lit up with a smile.)

I just might have reached home with the girl. Just three days ago, toward the end of reading class, Josephine called me over to her desk. "Mr. Coburn, look!" (pointing to the heading on her paper). I just smiled. My response was, "You sure are in a good mood!"

Although not related to my problem, I want to comment a bit on Josephine's behavior in the halls and especially with another teacher. Josephine's snippy, sassy behavior is very evident away from me and my classroom. One morning, Josephine was being "screamed" at in the hallway for her slowness in getting to class and for her poor attitude. In response, Josephine screamed back at the teacher (a behavior that I have never witnessed but have often thought was possible). Since then, I have seen her being reprimanded by the same teacher, time after time (like beating a dead horse).

Discussion. The teacher's remarks at the end of this case example are worth commenting on for several reasons. First, they help illustrate how context influences behavior. Which was the real Josephine? The Josephine in Mr. Coburn's class or the Josephine in the hallway with the other teacher? The answer is, of course, both. The difference is that Mr. Coburn transformed himself from a rather annoyed nag into an outgoing, friendly, informal teacher in relation to Josephine and helped to call the cooperative, interested Josephine into existence.

Another reason Mr. Coburn's remarks are worth commenting on is what they reveal about ecosystemic boundaries and the capacity of a change in one part of the ecosystem to influence the entire ecosystem. In theory, everything in Josephine's life is ecosystemically connected, and a change in any part of that ecosystem will affect every other part. However, just as when you throw a rock into a still pond and the ripples become less powerful as they spread from the center, changes in one part of an ecosystem do not affect every part with the same force. Nor is every part of an ecosystem affected the same way by a given change. The changes in Mr. Coburn's classroom influenced Josephine's relationship with him and were powerful enough to transform the problem situation in his classroom. They were obviously not potent enough to influence Josephine's relationship with the teacher yelling at her in the hallway. Although we have seen a number of cases in which changes at home, for example, influenced events in school, and vice versa, as a practical matter the functional boundary of an ecosystem is often the same as the setting in which the problem occurs, that is, the classroom, hallway, family, and so on.

Finally, it is worth pointing out that Mr. Coburn describes the teacher yelling at Josephine in the hallway as "beating a dead horse." This suggests to us that Mr. Coburn's experience with storming the back door has altered his view of Josephine as well as his view of how to approach problems.

In the following case example, a teacher describes the difficulty encountered trying to get a student to turn in his homework. After extensive attempts to solve the problem fail, and the boy still does not turn in his work, the teacher takes him aside—and talks about something else.

Case Example: Old Reliable

Alex is an eleven-year-old sixth-grader with average to above-average intelligence. He is quiet and shows proper respect to teachers and adults. He is not a disturbance in class. The problem stemmed from the fact that Alex did not do his assigned work, neither class work nor homework. He gave the impression of working but produced little or nothing by the end of the day.

Alex's mother and stepfather had been to school twice to express their concern with Alex's poor work habits. We had initiated a nightly homework sheet to check what Alex had completed during the day. This had limited success, because Alex would "forget" to do the homework assignments (which are incompleted daily assignments), or his mother would "forget" to sign the homework sheet.

Thursday I asked Alex for his homework and his signed homework sheet. He had not done his assignment, and the homework sheet had not been signed. Instead of reprimanding him as I usually did, I decided it was time to storm the back door. I took Alex aside and surprised him by saying that when he did his work I liked how neatly it was done. I also asked if he had noticed that I always called on him when he raised his hand. I told him I did so because I knew he would have a thoughtful answer. Alex was very pleased. [This is an example of storming the back door in the problem context. The teacher has chosen to talk with Alex about nonproblem (positive) topics in the problem situation.]

The results have been interesting. For the rest of Thursday, Alex worked diligently. He produced more than his usual output of work, but he still had work to take home. Alex seemed to raise his hand more and was extremely pleased when I would call on him. He always had the right answer. (We gave each other knowing smiles!)

On Friday, Alex was absent.

On Monday, Alex proudly turned in *twenty* overdue assignments. I made a big fuss and praised him for the completed assignments. That day he managed to complete all the morning assignments but still had the afternoon assignments as homework. I told him I knew he would get all the assignments finished and that they would be accurate and neat.

After only two days, it is hard to make a valid judgment, but I think I may be on the right track with Alex. Storming the back door by commenting about Alex's positive qualities has certainly brought about better results than harping on the problem.

Discussion. In addition to illustrating how the technique of storming the back door can be used in the problem context to change things, this case example shows how teachers can blend ecosystemic techniques with their own style. We do not generally recommend that teachers praise students when they begin to change in a way the teacher finds positive. However, in this instance, the teacher managed to blend a familiar approach (praising students for positive behavior) with a new technique—storming the back door. The best way for you to find out how such a blending of style and approaches might work is for you to try it in a problem situation and see what happens.

In our next case example, a teacher confronts one of the predictable crises faced by any teacher working with preadolescent girls.

Case Example: You Look Nice Today

It seems that about midway through sixth grade, young ladies begin to become very aware of their appearance and have an almost overpowering urge to alter their looks by applying several layers of eye, lip, and face makeup. There is also a great deal of peer pressure involved, and our recent social trends seem to support the idea of "enhancing" one's image. I commonly refer to this dilemma as AFS (artificial face syndrome). [Clearly, the teacher has a sense of humor and recognizes that he is coping with a social phenomenon.]

I consider this a problem in my classroom for several reasons. First, the application of makeup during class obviously interferes with study, lecture, and assignment work time. Second, girls are forming poor health habits. No thought is given to who borrows or uses whose combs, makeup brushes, mascara, or lip gloss. Third, this is a very sensitive subject with my administrator. A few years ago our school received some negative publicity concerning this very problem.

My first attempt to overcome the distraction caused by girls putting on makeup and combing their hair was the strong "I am the boss" approach, saying things like "You cannot do this in my classroom!" "The administration frowns on this type of behavior!" "That junk is harmful to your skin!" and "You cannot listen and put that junk on your face at the same time!" These outbursts only created other problems. Girls began to hide behind their books to apply makeup or asked several times during class to use the lavatory, where they would put on makeup.

Since the direct approach was not working, I decided to storm the back door. At the beginning of class, I took time to compliment students on how nice they looked. If I observed the girls exhibiting AFS at the end of class, I would again compliment them (sincerely, not sarcastically), from my desk, on how attractive they looked. Surprisingly, this did not disturb the other students at all. The girls soon stopped choosing to beautify themselves in my classroom, and artificial face syndrome rapidly disappeared.

My long-range plans are to continue to reinforce this behavior by taking special notice of these young ladies' appearance even though they are no longer applying cosmetics during class time.

Discussion. This case is a good example of how ecosystemic techniques can help make everyone a winner, instead of producing winners and losers. The teacher has been able to positively influence behavior that he considered negative for a number of good reasons. The girls involved had some positive attention paid to their appearance, an issue of great importance to preteens. The teacher changed. The girls changed. The situation was transformed.

In our next case example, we find yet another student failing to complete his work. In frustration, this teacher decides that what the classroom needs is a trusted lieutenant. Guess who becomes that able assistant?

Case Example: The Trusted Lieutenant

Raymond is an above-average student who was usually talking and making all of the other students laugh. He was the class clown. Because he wasted so much time in class, often much of his work was not completed for the next day—resulting in many 0s.

The usual sequence of events was this: Raymond would begin to talk to other students. I would tell him to quit disturbing others and to get back to his own work. Soon he was back to his usual talking, either during lessons or while students were being given time in class to work. Once again, I scolded him in front of the entire class. However, before long Raymond began talking to students around him again. Last straw for me! I would make him either stay in for gym or recess or write fifty times, "I will not disturb others."

Clearly something had to change. I decided the easiest thing for me to try would be storming the back door. I began by giving Raymond small jobs around the classroom. I also complimented him for being a neat worker and for other things he did well in my class. (He *is* quite smart.) Soon, when I had to leave the classroom for a few minutes at a time, I would leave Raymond in charge. At first, students complained that he was the person who usually fooled around. I responded by telling the class that I felt Raymond would do a fine job and that I considered him to be a "trusted lieutenant." They soon stopped complaining.

Little by little, I saw Raymond begin to change. He began to take pride in himself, knowing he could still get the attention he wanted but that it could be in a positive form. Raymond is getting into the routine of turning work in on time. This is much easier on Raymond as well as on me. I still compliment him and give him special duties, but not as often as in the beginning.

Discussion.   The teacher in this case example writes, "Little by little, I saw Raymond begin to change." Imagine how things must have looked to Raymond. This teacher stopped reprimanding him about being the "class clown," started complimenting him on things he did well, and, perhaps most dramatically of all, began to give him the responsibilities of a "trusted lieutenant." Judging from this teacher's description ("He began to take pride in himself, knowing he could still get the attention he wanted"), Raymond's problem behavior had been interpreted as an attention-getting device. Regardless of whether this interpretation was correct, it was not helping to change things. However, without challenging this interpretation, the teacher was able to use storming the back door as a way of figuring out what to do differently.

Review of the Essentials of Storming the Back Door

Storming the back door is a way of influencing the problem situation by focusing on some part of the ecosystem not directly related to the problem. For example, outside of the problem situation, the educator could create some positive interaction between her- or himself and the problem person—or in the problem situation, create some positive interaction not directly related to the problem. Storming the back door gives form to the ecosystemic idea that a change in any part of an ecosystem will influence every other part. The technique has several essential elements:

1. Identification of nonproblem aspects of the ecosystem that involve the person whose behavior is a problem
2. Identification of several possible positive attributes or behaviors of the problem person
3. Selection of a positive attribute or behavior
4. Formulation of a way of communicating a positive comment about the positive attribute or behavior
5. Communication of the positive comment

Procedure for Using Storming the Back Door

This activity is designed to help you think through a general procedure for using storming the back door.

1. Think of a person (or group) whose behavior is currently a problem for you. Imagine behaviors or attributes of that person (or group) or situations involving that person (or group) that are not a problem. (Examples: Alisa gets right down to work when she comes in in the morning. Gerald is well groomed. Tarina is cooperative on the playground.)

2. Select the behavior, attributes, or nonproblem situations that you believe you can most easily and genuinely comment on positively. (Example: Jackson turns in written work that is done neatly in language arts.)

3. Select the time and place in which you think it would be most natural for you to make your positive comment. (Example: as an aside after class.)

Now it is your turn. To try your hand at storming the back door, turn to the practice activity on page 177. This activity will help you prepare to apply storming the back door in a problem situation of your own.

9

Focusing on
What Is
Not a Problem

One of the best ways to construct solutions is to identify what the problem person does satisfactorily. In addition, it helps to recognize that your behavior in relation to the problem person is effective when that person is not causing a problem. It is common for a problem to obscure the effective and positive things that the people involved are already doing. As a sleuth, you should try never to overlook the resources and strengths present in the ecosystem. They represent the building blocks you can use to construct a solution. Too often educators fall victim to a needs-assessment mentality; that is, they search for weaknesses and deficiencies. The locating-exceptions technique is oriented toward a strength assessment; that is, what do I (we) do well that can be used as a foundation to do even better?

The Locating-Exceptions Technique

In art the difference between figure and ground is a basic distinction. We can use this distinction metaphorically to describe the relationship between problem and nonproblem behavior. When you have a problem with someone, it is normal that their problem behavior draws your attention and their nonproblem behavior is a relatively unnoticed backdrop. The locating-exceptions technique attempts to make nonproblem behavior the figure and draw attention to it, thus altering your perspective on the problem.

The effectiveness of focusing on exceptions to the problem "rule" in therapy has been described by de Shazer and Molnar

(1984b), de Shazer and others (1986), and Molnar and de Shazer (1987). By focusing on what is not a problem, the locating-exceptions technique is a logical extension of storming the back door. The difference between storming the back door and locating exceptions is a matter of degree. Storming the back door is an indirect, nonspecific technique designed to help you do something different and positive that is not associated with the problem behavior. The locating-exceptions technique is more focused. It asks you to consider closely the person whose behavior is a problem and to find ways to encourage their nonproblem behaviors without making reference to the problem.

Locating exceptions should not be confused with positive-reinforcement techniques, which tend to keep the focus only on the behavior of the problem person. The focus of the locating-exceptions technique is the entire ecosystem (which includes the problem situation). It is intended to influence the ecosystem and thus the problem behavior by shifting the emphasis from behaviors that are not acceptable to anything happening in the ecosystem that involves the problem person but that is not a problem. Asking yourself what is currently happening that you do not want to change may help you begin to locate exceptions to a problem "rule" that has been frustrating you (de Shazer, 1985).

Locating exceptions also offers you an opportunity to think clearly about what you are already doing that works. You might, for example, ask yourself, what am I doing that works with this student? At times when the problem behavior is not present, what am I doing with the student? What is the student doing? How can I use what I am already doing that is effective to learn how to become even more effective?

When you think about those things that you do not wish to change and those things that you are already doing that you do well, you will begin to see the differences between the problem situation and other situations. Often identifying these differences is the first step toward positive change.

Analysis of Case Examples

In our first case example, a teacher, irritated by a student's misbehavior during "in-between" times, thinks about the sort of situation in which the student does well. She realizes that the student does not disrupt when she is busy with an assignment. The teacher also recognizes that she knows how to keep the student busy. As a result, a way is found for the student to be "busy on an assignment" even during transition times.

Case Example: On Assignment

Joan often got into problems by poking others or calling others silly names during "in-between" times in class. These are times when we are finishing one activity and going on to another—collecting workbooks, putting materials away, lining up in class, and so on. I wanted to use an ecosystemic technique during these transition times to change this pattern. I decided that instead of focusing on the problem, I would try and identify what Joan did well. After some thought, I realized that when Joan was busy working on her assignments in class, she was only occasionally a problem. I realized that I needed to keep Joan occupied to have her stay out of trouble, and that I knew how to do it.

In the past I had gotten into the following pattern with Joan: (1) Work activity ends, and a new activity is about to begin; (2) Joan "acts up"; and (3) I discipline her. Although I usually restore order, Joan's behavior has never changed for very long. Once I realized that when Joan was occupied or busy, she was seldom involved in disruptive behavior, I knew I had located a useful "exception." I wanted to increase the times Joan could be kept busy, even if at these times we were not doing an assignment in class.

I decided I would tell Joan I had noticed how well she attended to her schoolwork and asked her to nod to me when she was ready to begin a new activity. I also decided I would try to acknowledge her readiness in some way. [The teacher has discovered that Joan is a good worker and does not disrupt others often if she is busy on a definite task. The teacher uses this knowledge about Joan and her own professional ability to devise ways to keep Joan busy during nonacademic transition times.]

While "locating exceptions" for Joan this week, these were some of the interactions that occurred:

1. When I was collecting reading workbooks, Joan's section

in class was finished, and the children were moving on to the learning center to select an activity. Joan nodded she was ready, and I asked her to straighten the workbooks on the shelf for me and then go on to the next activity. She did this, and there were no discipline problems at this transition time.

2. In lining up for art class this week (a time when there is a lot of activity going on—putting books away, passing out supplies), Joan nodded that she was ready, and I let her line up first. Others were still getting ready at their desks, and Joan seemed pleased at being the first person in line. This transition time again went well for her.

Joan seems happy at my acknowledgment of her readiness for a new activity, and I am happy I can encourage this cooperation from her rather than have to discipline her. Transition times are much smoother for us now that Joan is "busy with an assignment."

Discussion. By recognizing and building on both Joan's strengths and her own, the teacher in the "On Assignment" case example was successful in increasing the instances of Joan's nonproblem behavior.

In our next case example, a social worker uses locating exceptions to find a new way of thinking about a long-standing problem. It is interesting to see how nicely a common motivational device used by teachers (finding something a student is interested in and building on that) fits with locating exceptions.

Case Example: Accentuate the Positive

Jim, a nine-year-old boy repeating second grade, exhibited an academic lag, which I had decided (after an M-team staffing for suspected learning disabilities) was most likely the result of motivational problems. Jim had a good relationship with his teacher but showed little interest in academics and rarely completed written work unless prodded. Since Jim had shown little, if any, reaction to positive reinforcers, the team decided to ask Jim's mother to "fine" him for not completing daily assigned work. This met with no more success than anything else we had tried.

Finally, I asked the teacher if there was any subject area that triggered Jim's interest. After some thought, she remarked that he seemed to enjoy science, because he readily participated in and completed with no prodding what little written work there was for science lessons. I suggested that since Jim showed interest in science, the teacher might wish to use science material in reading and relate science to other academic areas as much as possible. I consulted with the teacher a week later, and she told me that she had obtained several science books as supplements for Jim. He was reportedly "looking at them."

I next began to reframe Jim's "unmotivated" behavior (termed passive and lazy by his teacher and mother) as his being "selectively interested." My goal as a case manager was to help Jim's teacher identify and build on what he did well in order to help the teacher learn to motivate him more effectively. I encouraged this very dedicated teacher to continue to observe Jim in class to see what he did that she would like to see continue. Although the results so far are not dramatic, I think we are all beginning to see Jim in a more positive light. This is encouraging us to continue looking for what he and his teacher do well so we can find an effective approach to improving his academic performance.

Discussion. Will Jim get more involved with his academic work as the result of his teacher's new focus on his interest in science? Will an effective way of motivating Jim be found by identifying what he and his teacher do well? We do not know. What we do know is that by considering Jim's interests and what he and his teacher do well, the people involved with him have been encouraged to keep looking for solutions. This encouragement is, in itself, an important aspect of using the locating-exceptions technique.

In our next case example, a kindergarten teacher discovers that one of the strengths of the problem student is working well at precisely structured activities. After having located this exception, the teacher proceeds to change things. This case example is a particularly good example of how a teacher was able comfortably to blend an ecosystemic technique with other more familiar techniques.

Case Example: Structuring Success

Celeste, a child in my morning kindergarten class, presented an ongoing problem. Celeste could be well described as a nonconformist. She preferred to do just as she pleased and tended to behave and to talk in a contrary fashion, disrupting the cooperative and harmonious atmosphere that generally existed in the class otherwise. She was alienating the other students. One could say she stuck out like a sore thumb.

Despite my efforts to set limits for Celeste, to encourage her sporadic attempts at improvement, and to teach her more constructive social skills, she had become increasingly defiant. She had begun to use bad language in class, to hit others even when not provoked, and to refuse to do what I told her to do.

I became very discouraged about Celeste's behavior and began to dread her arrival in class. I frequently phoned her mother, but this, too, was unproductive. Her mother said Celeste was fine at home—perhaps "because she and Celeste live alone, and Celeste has her complete attention."

Since I could not think of anything else to do, I began to look at Celeste's behavior in terms of the locating-exceptions technique to determine when her behavior was not a problem. Soon I observed that during some periods, when Celeste's work assignment was highly structured, she worked like a trouper, followed the directions for the work fairly well, and responded positively to my reminders and encouragement. The light dawned on me! Perhaps the rather informal framework of most of the kindergarten activities was not Celeste's forte, and I needed to structure activities much more precisely for Celeste—in a low-key fashion.

After identifying the highly structured work period as the situation in which the exceptions to Celeste's problem behavior usually occurred, I was able to develop a surprisingly effective strategy for increasing the nonproblem behavior. I began by discussing with Celeste the fact that she was doing a great job during work time. I wrote notes on her work papers that went home, praising her good work habits that day. I also set up a regimen of not only identifying and praising Celeste's increasingly cooperative behavior during work periods but also phoning her

mother with the good news. I asked her to tell Celeste I had phoned
and to relate the positive nature of our conversations.

[This teacher is applying what she has learned about
positively reinforcing desired behavior in the problem situation ("I
set up a regimen of not only identifying and praising Celeste's
increasingly cooperative behavior during work periods"). In
addition, she is doing something that has undoubtedly worked for
her in the past. She is telephoning a parent with good news. The
locating-exceptions technique helped this teacher think differently
about the problem and utilize her strengths to find a solution. It did
not mean the teacher had completely to change her style or her way
of thinking.]

This strategy worked so well that I began to feel better toward
Celeste and told her so. I praised her improvement and suggested
we try to carry it over into other activities in addition to work time.
I told her she would next need to listen carefully and to follow my
very special rules for her for the independent activity (play) time.

Then I set up a highly structured situation for her during
play period, defining her materials, interactions, and location in the
room and giving her directions for use of the materials—just as I
had done for the work period. She had her ups and downs with this
at first. I responded by focusing attention on her successes and
eliminating some of the variables in the situation to make her
framework even more structured.

To summarize, with some setbacks from time to time, I have
been able to expand the highly structured environment for Celeste
to include most of the kindergarten activities. Her mother is also
cooperating in phoning me regularly to obtain the good news to
relate to Celeste, as well as to receive pointers in using the locating-
exceptions technique at home.

Celeste is learning at an above-average rate in most areas of
the kindergarten skills. Every day at dismissal time, I quietly ask her
who was her best friend in school that day. Although ten days ago
she refused even to answer that question, lately she names someone
every day. Celeste is beginning to feel good about herself, and she
now smiles occasionally in school. I feel much more warmly toward
her now. A feeling of success seems to be contagious. Even her

mother expresses her pleasure to me at "finally being able to reach Celeste!"

Discussion. In this case example and in our first case example in this chapter, the exception located was the student's satisfactory behavior in well-defined and structured situations. It would be tempting to draw the conclusion that when students disrupt during unstructured times, what they need is structure. We see nothing wrong with attempting to structure the time of students who disrupt during relatively unstructured times. This is not, however, an ecosystemic rule of any sort. Ecosystemically, what is important in these two case examples is that in both cases the teacher changed something, and that change was associated with other positive changes in the classroom. We caution you against turning the particular form a successful ecosystemic technique took in one instance (for example, structuring a child's time more closely) into a general rule to be applied under similar circumstances (for example, saying that whenever a child disrupts during transition times, the recommended solution is to make that child's time more structured).

Ecosystemic techniques are intended to help produce change. Each problem is considered in terms of its own characteristics. This is what helps to distinguish an ecosystemic approach from a diagnostic approach. A diagnostic approach attempts to place problem behaviors into categories and to find rules for responding to those categories of behavior. From an ecosystemic perspective, it is quite likely that the teachers in our first and third case examples in this chapter could have located different exceptions to the problem behavior, acted based on these exceptions, and come up with equally positive changes.

Our final case example in this chapter is unusual because it is the only case example in the book that involves a therapist. This case example, first reported by Lindquist, Molnar, and Brauckmann (1987), illustrates how the relationship between a parent and the school can help maintain or help change a problem situation in the classroom. In this instance, the therapist helped a mother, her son, and a teacher find and build on school behaviors that were positive and that they did not want to change.

Case Example: Don't Call Me; I'll Call You

The mother of a middle school student requested therapy for her son because he was causing numerous problems in school, and the teacher was calling her about him three or four times a week. The student did not do his homework or completed it but did not turn it in. He got into arguments and fistfights with other students and was described as having an explosive temper. The student had been referred for therapy in the past for school-related problems. [Here we see the common pattern of the people involved with a problem being really involved. A teacher who is willing to take the time and energy to call a parent three or four times a week is dedicated indeed. For her part, the mother has been receiving a steady stream of complaints for a long time and is perhaps feeling as puzzled and frustrated as her son's teachers. Despite the energy taken up with this problem, the current focus is not helping to change things.]

The therapist decided to use a series of ecosystemic interventions designed to address the student's school problems and to change the pattern of interaction that had been established between the school and the family. Previously, the school had contacted the mother, and the discussion had been about the problems with the child. As a part of therapy, this pattern was altered: first, by having the mother contact the school instead of waiting for the school to call her when her son was causing problems; second, by changing the discussion between the mother and the teacher from a discussion of the problems her son was causing to a discussion of what was happening when he was not getting in trouble and how to increase those exceptions. [The therapist has initiated two significant changes. First, by having the mother contact the school to inquire about her son, the therapist has suggested a behavior likely to be interpreted positively by the teacher. Second, by having the mother talk with the teacher about exceptions to the problem behavior, the therapist has given the mother and the teacher something positive to talk about—probably for the first time in a long time.]

At the close of the first therapy session, during which the information about the problem was obtained, the mother was asked to telephone her son's teacher prior to the next session and to talk with him about what was happening when her son was not getting in trouble in school. The mother was asked to gather this information so she could relate it to the therapist in the next session.

During the next session, the mother recounted all of the things the teacher said he had observed when her son was not getting in trouble. The student was also asked what he had noticed about those times. The therapist then held a detailed discussion with the student and his mother about the circumstances under which the student did not get into trouble. The mother was then asked to contact the teacher again to thank him for the information he had been able to supply and to let him know it had been helpful. She was also asked to discuss with the teacher how he accounted for the good days and to find out if he had made any further observations about what was happening when things were going well. [Notice how the teacher's role has been shifted from bearer of bad news to consultant on how to increase the instances of positive behavior. This is probably a much more personally and professionally satisfying role for the teacher.]

When the student's behavior had improved to the point of being acceptable, the therapist discussed with the student and his mother how they would be able to recognize a bad day as only a temporary setback. After discussing the ways they would do this, the mother was asked to talk with the student's teacher about the likelihood of there being some bad days in the future and how he might recognize them as minor setbacks. [Here the therapist combines predicting a relapse (Chapter Ten) with locating exceptions in order to support the changes being made.]

Throughout the course of therapy, the format described above was used. The mother was asked to contact the school and not wait to be contacted. She was asked by the therapist to obtain information from the teacher about exceptions to the problems, that is, situations in which her son was not in trouble; how the teacher accounted for these exceptions; and how to increase those situations in which things were going well. When the student's behavior improved, the teacher was asked how he accounted for the change.

The technique of locating exceptions helped establish a cooperative relationship between the family and the school and respected and utilized the knowledge and information that the school and the family could provide.

Discussion. This case example demonstrates how important it is to establish a framework for cooperation in problem situations. Although we can assume that the mother and the teacher in this example had good intentions, the problem-focused relationship they had was defeating them. We can understand why a mother might not call a school if the result was a recitation of all the problems her son was causing. We can also understand why a teacher who was having problems with a child might interpret the mother's not contacting the school as disinterest. By providing a concrete and positive focus for mother-teacher conversations, the therapist was able to encourage the mother to contact the teacher. With a positive focus instead of a problem focus, the mother and the teacher were able to establish a cooperative relationship and to work together for a constructive change in the student's behavior.

Review of the Essentials of Locating Exceptions

Locating exceptions is an attempt to identify the positive and functional behaviors of a person. It emphasizes increasingly the instances of positive behaviors rather than focuses on how to decrease problem behavior. The result of using locating exceptions is often a generally more positive attitude toward the person whose behavior is problematic.

The essential elements of locating exceptions are:

1. Identification of situations when the problem behavior is not occurring
2. Awareness of those things that distinguish situations in which the problem behavior does not occur from situations in which the problem behavior does occur
3. Selection of a nonproblem behavior or nonproblem situation that it appears would be easiest to increase in frequency
4. Formulation of an approach to increasing the time spent in the nonproblem situation or increasing the incidence of nonproblem behavior

Procedure for Locating Exceptions

This activity is designed to help you think through a general procedure for locating exceptions.

1. Think of a person whose behavior is currently a problem for you. Identify the situation(s) in which this person does not exhibit this problem behavior. Identify the differences between the problem and nonproblem situations. (Example: Rory does not cause problems when he collects lunch money for me. In this situation he has responsibility for doing something, and he and I cooperate. When Rory talks to the children around him during quiet seat work and I tell him to stop, he becomes defiant, and we usually end up yelling at each other.)

2. What behaviors, qualities, characteristics, and so on of the person whose behavior is a problem would you like to see more of? (Example: I would like to increase the amount of personal responsibility Rory has in the classroom, and I would like to spend more time cooperating instead of fighting with him.)

3. Describe how you are different in nonproblem situations. What are you already doing to encourage nonproblem behaviors? (Example: I often comment to Rory, when I ask him to collect the lunch money, that it is nice to have such a responsible and trustworthy student to help me out.)

4. Formulate a plan for increasing the nonproblem behavior using what you know about (1) the characteristics of nonproblem situations, (2) the behaviors and qualities that you want to encourage, and (3) what you are already doing that works. (Example: I will stop commenting to Rory when he whispers during quiet seat work. Instead, I will begin to make general comments to Rory throughout the day about his trustworthiness and sense of responsibility. I will communicate as clearly as I can that since I trust him I know that he has good reasons for his behavior.)

Now it is your turn. To try your hand at locating exceptions, turn to the practice activity on page 178. This activity will help you prepare to apply locating exceptions in a problem situation of your own.

10

Predicting and
Handling Relapses

In Chapter One, we discussed the difficulty of changing in chronic problem situations. By definition, the interactions in such situations have occurred repeatedly for some time. Therefore, it is not surprising that even after there has been an initial change, the problem often reappears. Interestingly, as we saw in some of the case examples, the return to old, familiar ways of interacting sometimes began by a teacher praising a student for improved behavior (even though praise had not been helpful in the past) and the student responding by reverting to the original problem behavior. In other case examples, even though the educator maintained the new way of interacting, the original problem behavior reemerged. Predicting a relapse is one way of planning for or responding to the reappearance of a problem behavior.

The Predicting-a-Relapse Technique

In well-established patterns of behavior, it is to be expected that, after some change, there may be some recurrence of the old behavior or behavior pattern. Family therapists often use the technique of predicting a relapse to help their clients regard the reappearance of a problem behavior as a part of the normal progress toward a solution instead of as a failure. By describing the reappearance of the problem behavior as a temporary relapse that is normal and expected, everyone in the problem situation can continue to cooperate and maintain the change by seeing the relapse as the exception and the changes as the rule. Thus a relapse becomes a sign that the normal processes of positive change are occurring rather than a cause for alarm.

As you read through the case examples in this chapter, you will notice that predicting a relapse is always used in combination with one or more other ecosystemic techniques. This is because predicting a relapse is used to support the changes made once the change process has already begun.

To illustrate the use of predicting a relapse in combination with reframing, positive connotation of motive, positive connotation of function, and symptom prescription, we rely once again on the example of the child blurting out answers, while the teacher tries to ignore the blurting out. If the teacher has reframed the student's blurting out answers as manifestations of the student's intense enthusiasm, then predicting a relapse might sound like this: "I expect that your enthusiasm is going to continue to show itself from time to time in unexpected ways, including blurting out answers. That is to be expected from a person as energetic as you. Besides, when you blurt out an answer from time to time, it will help me remember how lucky I am to have such an enthusiastic student."

If the teacher has used positive connotation of motive to connote the motive of a student who blurts out answers as a desire to express interest in the lessons, then predicting a relapse might sound something like this: "I am genuinely pleased to have a student as interested in my lessons as you are. I would not be surprised if you sometimes call out answers out of turn. Given the intensity of your interest, that would be normal."

If the teacher has used positive connotation of function to explain that the student's blurting out of answers was a way of encouraging her or him to rethink her or his methods of classroom questioning, then predicting a relapse might sound like this: "I have followed my usual routine of classroom questioning for some time. Old habits die hard. If you begin to call out answers again, that will be a sign to me that I have had a relapse and need to remember to try a variety of ways to ask questions."

If the teacher has used symptom prescription and asked the child who blurts out answers to write out a "blurt gram" before saying anything, then predicting a relapse may sound like this: "It may be hard at first to get used to writing out blurt grams, so I would not be surprised if you still blurt out an answer from time to time before writing your blurt gram."

Because relapses are such a normal part of changing, it is possible to predict that they will happen. As the case studies in this chapter illustrate, it is possible to use the technique before a relapse has occurred by simply predicting to the person that it would be normal if it were to happen; or, if a relapse actually occurs, to tell the person after the fact that this is a normal part of change, and "it could have been predicted." It is possible that in your own way you may find that a problem situation has begun to change without your having used any particular technique. In these instances, predicting a relapse can also be helpful to you as a way of encouraging the positive developments to continue.

Analysis of Case Examples

In the following case example, a teacher uses several ecosystemic ideas (including cooperation, reframing, using the students' language, and predicting a relapse) to solve the problem of two bright girls who finished their work and then disrupted the class.

Case Example: Just Wondering When the Relapse Would Happen

In a Spanish 1 class, I have two girls who are very good students. They were in Spanish together in the middle school and are good friends. They would master new material very quickly and then cause a problem with talking, giggling, and writing notes. This activity was not done only between themselves. They included others who could not afford not to pay attention. I had tried to redirect their energy by giving them extra materials, but they would lose interest in these materials and soon start to disrupt the class with their antics. I did not want to punish them because they are good students, and I did not want to turn them off to Spanish. I wanted to redirect their energies and use their ability in Spanish to benefit them and the rest of the class.

I decided to ask both girls to see me after school. When they came in, I could tell that they were expecting to be punished or talked to about their behavior. Instead, I complimented them on their fine grades, neat work, and eagerness in the classroom. They seemed a bit surprised. They relaxed even more when I used a few slang words I had heard them use before.

I went on to explain to the girls that I could tell that they did not need to spend as much time on new material as many of the other students, and I asked if they would not mind helping me by working individually with the rest of the class. They loved the idea.

I also knew that this was not enough for them. I asked them if they would be interested in making worksheets and developing learning activities for use in class when they were not needed as tutors and felt they understood the classwork. They almost had a fit with excitement, trying to decide which ideas to put into effect first. I told them we would meet during their study hall to plan which material they would use during class time to prepare learning activities. The girls left feeling excited about the use of the unproductive class time.

The following day, it was great not having to scold the girls for talking. I asked them to help students with their worksheets, as I was doing the same. They have since developed five worksheets and a variety of games to help other students understand new material better and faster.

For two and one-half weeks after our initial talk, the girls' behavior in the classroom presented no problem; in fact, they were excited, eager, and truly helpful. However, the novelty is wearing off. I can sense a bit of disenchantment or lack of motivation, and there have been very minor recurrences of their problem behavior.

Given that problem patterns are persistent, I was expecting a relapse. Therefore, I decided to discuss the relapse with them and to comment that relapses are normal. Once again, I decided to use their language when talking with them.

The first thing I did was to meet with them and praise them again for their accomplishments. I told them that I thought their behavior in Spanish class was "totally awesome" and "megagreat." I also told them that I had been anticipating a relapse and was wondering just when it would happen. I explained to them that since a small relapse had occurred, I wanted to be sure that they understood that it was normal to fall back into old patterns of behavior once in a while. I also told them that I had total confidence in them and that I knew they would be back on track very soon. I tried to make them feel that their relapse was okay and normal and that they had not failed. Using the girls' figurative language really helped me to communicate with them. Since I have done this intuitively in the past, it fits very well with my style.

After our talk, the girls felt better about their relapse. I thought it was time to give them another new project. I said to them, "I can tell you girls totally enjoy Spanish because your grades are so phenomenal. I bet you must be super proud of yourselves for the great worksheets and projects you have completed for the whole class. It is also neat helping your friends understand the Spanish that comes so easily to you, isn't it? You are probably waiting for another project, so tomorrow start on South American youth music." The girls left the room feeling good about their progress, not poorly about the relapse, and excited about their new project. I felt great, although a bit skeptical about what the future would hold.

It has been eight school days since my talk with the girls. They seem to have renewed interest in doing additional classroom projects. Up to now, there has not been a second relapse. They know it is possible or even probable. If one occurs, I am ready for it! One of the things I appreciate most about the predicting-a-relapse technique is that it certainly decreases the amount of confrontations with students per day and per class.

Discussion. This case example not only shows how to use the technique of predicting a relapse after a relapse has already started, but also makes an important point about the effect this technique can have on the person or people with whom it is being used. ("The girls left the room feeling good about their progress, not poorly about the relapse"). Commonsensically, it might be expected that to point out a relapse would interfere with the cooperation established in the problem situation. Paradoxically, pointing out the relapse, but describing it as normal, supports the cooperation as well as the changes that have taken place in the problem situation.

Case Example: The Conscientious Calculator

Another way of using the technique of predicting a relapse is to predict one before the relapse occurs, as the teacher in "The Conscientious Calculator" did (Chapter Seven) when working with the student who wrote out all of the computations for every math problem.

After using the technique of sympton prescription and encouraging the student not only to write out all of the steps of every math problem but also to keep them in a special notebook and show them to the math teacher, the student stopped after a few days because she said it "takes too long."

Before the student had a relapse, the teacher predicted one by commenting, "you might need to write out some steps as you go along. In fact, I would really be surprised if you did not need to occasionally. So please be sure to write it down when you need to."

The teacher reported that the student continued to do most of the computing in her head and made only a few notations in the notebook.

Discussion. The teacher in this case used symptom prescription to encourage the student to engage in the problem behavior differently. When predicting the relapse, she was able to maintain her cooperative position and predict a reemergence of the old computing behavior by saying it would be surprising if the student did not need to write out some problems on occasion. The teacher could be consistent with the original symptom prescription and encourage the student to write out problems from time to time as needed.

As this case example illustrates, predicting a relapse can often forestall one. If a relapse occurs after having been predicted, it can be viewed as normal and temporary. In this way, progress can be enhanced rather than inhibited, because the relapse is seen as a sign of progress.

The next case example illustrates how predicting a relapse was used with two students to describe to them the reappearance of the problem behavior as a normal occurrence.

Case Example: Concerned Classmates

In this case example from Chapter Five, two students who attended a learning center for academic remediation would arrive at the center telling tales of what the "other guy" had done wrong during the day in the regular classroom. The teacher initially described their putdowns and telling on each other as a counterproductive game of one-upmanship.

The teacher decided to use positive connotation of the students' motives for "getting on" one another and began commenting to them about their caring and concern for one another. He described the boys' behavior as being motivated by their desire to help each other learn and get ahead. This was effective in altering the boys' behavior for a week and a half (nine visits to the center). Then one of the other teachers noticed that the old behaviors had started to reappear.

In describing his use of predicting a relapse, the teacher reported that he smilingly approached the two boys and said, "I am not surprised that you are still sacrificing your interests for each other. In fact, I predicted it to your teacher. Old ways of showing concern such as yours are not easily changed."

Discussion. The teacher has positively connoted the boys' behavior as being motivated by their concern for each other. When the old behavior reappears, he tells the boys its reappearance was to be expected because old ways (of showing concern) are not easily changed. In doing this, he defines both the old and the new ways of behaving as concern. In effect, what the teacher is saying is that although the old behavior has temporarily reappeared, the boys' concern for each other has never wavered. Thus, he is able to maintain his positive focus and encourage the constructive changes that have occurred in the boys' behavior.

Case Example: Walking to Work

In this case example from Chapter Seven, the teacher described a student who would walk around in the room, talk to other students, and not finish her work. Using the technique of symptom prescription, the teacher had altered the problem situation satisfactorily, and the student's behavior changed. There was a lapse in time between the end of the regular school year and the beginning of summer school. When the student began summer school, the teacher discovered that the problem behavior did not reappear. The student was still sitting and doing her work instead of walking around. Nevertheless, the teacher decided to predict a relapse in order to support this positive change.

The teacher incorporated her original symptom prescription about the student needing to walk sometimes with predicting a relapse by telling the student that it would be normal if she found it necessary to walk around a bit before starting to work. In this case, the student did do some walking, but according to the teacher, it was minimal.

Discussion. This case example raises an important point regarding the effect predicting a relapse can have on the person using it. By predicting that there may be a reappearance of the original problem behavior, when this occurs it helps the educator remember the changes that have taken place. If your expectation is that the problem behavior will never reappear, then seeing it again can be very discouraging. Expecting a relapse and even predicting one can help you maintain your new way of responding by encouraging you to keep your focus on the changes that have occurred and to treat the relapse as a normal part of the change process.

In our next case example, a very dedicated teacher had been unable to find a way to stop a student from "organizing" and to get him to start in on his work. After changing the problem situation by reframing the student's behavior and prescribing the symptom, the teacher follows up by predicting a relapse.

Case Example: The Organization Man

Andre is a capable sixth-grader who accomplished less than expected. He rarely was prepared for class and had a lax attitude toward his work.

Since Andre was assigned to my homeroom, I had him for

study hall. It was extremely annoying that although he had a lot of work to do, he spent most of his time fooling with papers or things and not getting to work. It was not unusual for him to spend more than half of study hall "organizing" at his desk or locker.

I had placed restrictions on him such as "have your work out by one o'clock" or "you may have only one trip to your locker" or "in ten minutes, bring up what you have done." He had been asked to work in other teachers' rooms so that he could work on their subjects. I had made calls home and had had four conferences with his parents this year. I had even pulled his desk alongside mine.

In an attempt to reframe the situation, I pointed out Andre's obvious concern about organization by telling him that I was glad to see he was so concerned about organizing his things. I said some students cared very little about how their materials were arranged. I told him that he should take as much time as he felt was necessary to get things in good order before he started working.

Andre looked like he had seen a ghost. He sat in shock for a while after I left. He then proceeded to get to work. This has continued for several class periods, even though he does not have study hall every day.

After about three days of this new behavior, I commented to Andre that I had noticed he was completing a lot of work in study hall. I told him it would be normal if, occasionally, he found himself using his study hall time to organize. I even said that I would not be surprised if he had one of his organizing sessions within the next two study periods. In those two study periods he did not spend excess time organizing, however. It is like dealing with a new student.

Discussion.   This case example illustrates once again how using ecosystemic techniques helps create a cooperative relationship between educators and students. If Andre should spend a study period or two organizing, this will not be characterized as a defeat by the teacher or as a victory by Andre. It will only be a normal part of the cooperative process of change. The teacher's last sentence, "It is like dealing with a new student," is illuminating. We imagine that the student feels the same way about his teacher.

In our final case example, a teacher finds a way to use predicting a relapse with an entire class.

Case Example: The Relapse Agreement

All students enter the building at 8:35 A.M. and proceed directly to their classrooms.

My students unload their book bags in the hall outside of the room. They dispose of jackets, empty book bags, and other unneeded materials in their lockers. Materials needed for the day are brought into the classroom, and at that point, the students' preparation time begins. They have approximately ten minutes to review their assignments for the day and copy down the assignments for the next day before I begin to take the lunch and milk count.

It was during this ten-minute preparation time that most students would begin walking around the room and talking with one another. I usually moved around the room, reminding the students again and again to use their preparation time wisely. Many did not get their new assignments copied, and the talking sometimes spilled over into the lunch-and-milk-count time. This made it necessary for me to raise my voice and ask the students to be quiet during lunch and milk count so that I could hear.

The situation was not out of hand, but it made me feel like I was spending the first ten minutes of each day playing policeman. I did not like this somewhat negative way of beginning each day, and I am sure the students did not like it either.

I decided to reframe the students' behavior beginning on the next Monday. On Monday morning, I waited until after preparation time, lunch and milk count, and music class. Then I explained to the students that I had been beginning to get angry with them until I realized that they needed a time to visit with one another. I then went on to say that I knew there were many things that happened after school and in the morning before school that they liked to share with one another, and that I would allow them to visit freely with one another until lunch and milk count if they would then be very quiet so I could hear. I said I would provide a different time during the day to copy the new assignments.

As I was doing the reframing with the students, the most

obvious reaction was the smiles. I am sure some were smiling because they were happy to hear that they could now visit without having to listen to my nagging. But I had a very strong feeling that many were smiling because they found what they were hearing hard to believe.

On Tuesday I stationed myself outside the classroom door so that I could supervise the hallway, greet the students, and, most of all, observe the new situation in the classroom.

The students appeared more active and louder than usual. However, when I walked into the room after the tone had sounded to take the lunch and milk count, there was complete silence.

The students seemed to settle down and become more quiet as the week came to an end. I observed many students limiting their visiting and getting their new assignments copied before the lunch and milk count.

On Thursday of the second week, there was a lot of talking during the lunch and milk count. I decided it was time to use the technique of predicting a relapse. I stopped, asked for their attention, and spent about three to four minutes reviewing what we had talked about on Monday of the previous week. Then I added that it was quite normal for the old talking behavior to come back occasionally. I offered to remind them on those occasions about our agreement. When I continued the lunch and milk count, they were completely quiet.

Now, when it becomes a little noisy during lunch and milk count, all I have to say is "remember our agreement," and it is quiet, and the students have had no problems getting their new assignments copied each day.

Discussion. In this case example, the teacher manages to solve an irritating chronic problem by acknowledging that his students had good reasons for their behavior and by treating them as good-faith negotiators when they had a relapse. Predicting a relapse helped this teacher find a way of talking to students in a friendly and cooperative way. By so doing, the teacher supported and encouraged the positive change in the classroom.

Review of the Essentials of Predicting a Relapse

Predicting a relapse is a technique; however, it also embodies an attitude toward the reappearance of a problem behavior. In essence, describing the reappearance of a problem behavior as a temporary relapse is a reframing. Instead of the behavior heralding yet another failure, it is interpreted as a sign that something normal in the change process has occurred.

It is not necessary to predict a relapse in advance. Some teachers have, however, found it helpful to be skeptical of a student's new nonproblem behavior. In these instances, a teacher might tell a student that it would not be surprising if he or she relapsed into the old problem behavior. After all, it is hard to change old habits. Each teacher must decide for him- or herself if it is appropriate to use predicting a relapse in advance of any recurrence of the problem.

When you have not predicted a relapse of the problem behavior and the behavior recurs, your tone will be very important. Predicting a relapse should not be accompanied by a tone of voice or any other nonverbal cue that you knew the person could not really change for the better. Remember, predicting a relapse is designed to focus on and encourage the positive changes that have occurred, not to call them into question. Therefore, your tone should be mild and understanding and should clearly communicate that you see what has happened as an understandable but temporary setback. The student should learn from his or her exchange with you that setbacks are normal, that other setbacks may occur, but that the process of positive change is moving ahead.

11

If at First
You Don't Succeed:
Guidelines for Trying Again

Sometimes case examples in books sound like fairy stories and have the quality of being too good to be true. Although we have included some case examples in which the person would have liked more change and others in which there were setbacks or other difficulties, for the most part we have used case examples in which the person was successful, and the report focuses on the successful outcome, not the details of the glitches along the way. We recognize, life being what it is, that glitches are inevitable. In order to help you apply these ideas in a real-life situation, we have attempted to anticipate some of the questions you might have. The following are guidelines to use if you have tried a technique, and it did not work.

1. Wait. Since the ideas in this book suggest responding in a chronic problem situation quite differently than you have responded in the past, it is important to allow your changed response to have an effect on the chronic problem pattern. See, for example, the case example "The Conscientious Calculator" in Chapter Seven, in which a teacher waited three days before a change in the student's behavior took place that the teacher considered progress.

2. Observe. In chronic problem situations, we are often more acutely aware of the problem and its details than we are of the initial small signs that signal change is taking place. It is therefore important to look for these small initial signs of change so as not to miss them and think the intervention has failed. See, for example, the case example "Distant Drums" in Chapter Three, in which a

156

teacher thought the intervention had not only failed but also made the situation worse. However, he continued to look for and did observe positive changes.

3. Repeat the intervention. Check to make sure that you are using the technique you have chosen properly. Review the "Essentials of . . ." section at the end of the chapter in which that technique is discussed and repeat the practice activity for that technique in the "Resource" section. If you are confident you are using the technique properly, then repeat the intervention. Chronic problems consist of stable patterns. Just as it is necessary to allow some time for the intervention to disrupt the pattern, it may also be necessary to repeat the intervention in order to disrupt the pattern. As some of the case examples illustrate, people are sometimes taken aback initially by the intervention because the new way of responding is so different. The person may have to hear the intervention or experience your new response more than once to grasp it. See, for example, the case example "Lazy Troublemakers or Best Friends?" in Chapter Four.

4. Try another technique. The techniques described in this book are not problem specific, so, for example, it cannot be said that if you are working on a problem situation in which a student talks out of turn, you should use reframing. Rather, the success of these techniques depends on the interaction of the person using the technique, the person with whom it is being used, and the context of the problem. If you have tried reframing, and it has not worked, you might be more comfortable with this particular person, in this particular situation, trying symptom prescription or positive connotation of motive. See, for example, the case example "The Talker" in Chapter Three, in which a teacher tried three different strategies.

5. Did you use the other person's language? The degree to which you can communicate the intervention using the other person's figurative language may affect how quickly and to what extent they grasp the intervention. If you have tried to positively connote the function of a person's behavior, for example, and they misunderstood, saying it again in their language might make the difference between initiating change and having little or no effect. See, for example, the case example "The Quarterback Sneak" in

Chapter Three, in which a teacher used football metaphors to communicate with three boys who were on a community football team.

6. Have you attempted to look at the situation from the other person's perspective? To help you do this, you might try to imagine how that person would describe your behavior. You might also try to imagine how that person would reframe your behavior or what they might find as a positive motive for your behavior. For a good example of putting oneself in the other person's shoes, see the case example "Belligerent Bad Guy or Awkward Adolescent?" in Chapter Four, in which a teacher imagined how awkward he would feel attempting to do the dance routine his students were working on and realized the student who was causing problems was as big as the teacher and might also feel awkward.

7. Did the technique you chose allow you to act honestly and sincerely in relation to the person? If you chose to use reframing with a person in a problem situation, and you believe the reframing is a lie, it is unlikely to work. Choose a different technique that will allow you to act honestly and sincerely. See, for example, the case example "Unwanted Attention" in Chapter Two, in which a teacher chooses not to use reframing with a colleague because he fears he could not use it without sounding sarcastic. He uses a different technique instead.

8. After some initial change, did you revert to your old pattern of responding? As some of the case examples illustrated, after some initial success, the educator reverted to the old pattern of responding, and the person the educator was working with reverted as well. If this has happened, repeat the intervention that brought about the initial change. See, for example, the case example "Inanimate Object or Enthusiastic Girl?" in Chapter Six, in which the teacher was successful at changing the problem situation. She began responding to the student the way she had formerly by praising the student, who then reverted to her former problem behavior of doing nothing. When the teacher once again positively connoted the function of the student's behavior, the student started participating again.

9. Is there another part of the ecosystem that can be involved? Often it is sufficient to work only with one part of the ecosystem.

At times, however, it may be helpful to include other parts of the ecosystem, for example, teacher aides, a group of students, or the entire class. It may at times also be helpful to look at a larger ecosystem such as the school and to include an administrator, or to move to the ecosystem that includes the home and the school and to involve a parent. See, for example, the case example "A Serious Student in Comedian's Clothing" in Chapter Six, in which a teacher involved two teacher aides, or the case example "The Sacrificial Lamb" in Chapter Six, in which a school counselor worked with a remedial teacher. See also the case example "Sad Sarah—with Good Reason" in Chapter Four, in which a teacher involved the child's mother and her former schoolteacher to help solve the problem.

All of the case examples in this book are based on our students' work. They have reported that the more they used the techniques, the easier it was for them, and they noticed that they began thinking about problem situations and potential solutions differently. In the last chapter, there is a description of our students' experiences over a semester's time, as they first learned ecosystemic techniques and then applied them in their classrooms and schools. They found that if they kept sleuthing, they were usually able to come up with a creative solution. This may be your experience as well.

12

Refining Your Skills
in Solving Problems
and Changing Behavior

When you begin implementing an ecosystemic approach, it will be helpful to remember that the focus is on change. In some ways, the entire message of *Changing Problem Behavior in Schools* can be summed up in one sentence: When you want something to change, you must change something. Each of the techniques we have described represents a different way of helping you change a problem situation by changing your perspective or your behavior or both.

We have no illusions that change is necessarily easy. There is plenty of research evidence to suggest, for example, that it takes much more data to overturn an existing belief than it does to sustain it (Taylor and Brown, 1988). As we explained in Chapter One, there are a variety of reasons why not changing in a problem situation is understandable. You do not arrive in school as a blank slate. You arrive as a person with characteristics shaped in part by the unique experiences of your life as well as experiences you share with others of the same race, gender, and social class. The interaction between the characteristics you bring to your work as an educator and the social context of your school cannot help but influence your point of view as you go about your job. Reflecting on the history of your own development and the social context in which you work can help you to understand why you find it difficult to change in a given problem situation. It can also help you to change by helping you put your perspective in perspective.

Putting Your Perspective in Perspective

A concrete way to become more aware of your perspective (and begin to change it at the same time) is to ask yourself the following questions: (1) From the perspective of the person with whom I have a problem, how might my behavior be interpreted? (2) What is the difference between my interpretation of my behavior and the interpretation of the person with whom I have a problem? (3) What different behavior(s) on my part (that are acceptable to me) might be interpreted as a positive change by the problem person?

Consider our example of the student who blurts out answers and the teacher who tries to ignore the behavior. If the teacher asked him- or herself our three questions, the answers might be something like this: (1) From the perspective of the student, my behavior might be interpreted as not caring what the student has to say or as my being more concerned with classroom rules and regulations than with encouraging a student who is interested in the subject matter. (2) My understanding of my behavior is that I am trying to conduct effective lessons in which each child learns what is taught. From the student's perspective, perhaps I am seen as not interested in what the student has to say and as being primarily concerned with rules and not with substance. (3) Maybe if I comment to the student that I recognize his or her enthusiasm about the subject matter, complain to the student that I often feel boxed in by rules and ask for some help in figuring a way out, or simply ask the student to call on people after I ask a question, the student's perception of me and the situation will begin to change.

If you are able to respond to the questions we have raised, it may be easier for you to see a variety of perspectives on the problem situation. This may not immediately produce an acceptable solution; it will, however, increase the likelihood that you will see more *possible* things to try out than previously. One invariable characteristic of a problem situation is that the people involved cannot see a way out. They believe that they have tried everything they know how to do, and they feel trapped. In cases like these, anything that helps you think of new possibilities has already made a big difference.

We have noticed that frequently, once something has been changed, a new situation emerges that is neither the problem nor exactly the foreseen solution. Often this changed situation is acceptable to those involved. Sometimes it is not regarded as optimal, but it is recognized as an improvement and as a hopeful development. We call this a negotiated solution. Without saying so explicitly, the people involved in the problem situation have negotiated a satisfactory modus vivendi that they can support.

It is our hope that being curious about your own perspective on a problem situation will make it easier for you to be curious about how the other person or people involved interpret what is happening and that this curiosity will help you learn to think and act differently. In some ways, a problem behavior is nothing more than a message to you that something has to change. The mystery is which perspective(s) will best help illuminate potential changes. Problem situations offer you the opportunity to play master sleuth and to think new thoughts. They are excellent devices for promoting your own creativity.

Analyzing Your Creativity

One of our underlying assumptions is that people have the knowledge they need to solve their problems. When stymied in a chronic problem situation, they may have temporarily forgotten what they know, or perhaps they have not quite put together all the pieces in a particular problem situation in a helpful way.

Before using any of the techniques that we have described in this book, it might be helpful for you to do some reminiscing. Think about problem situations you have faced in the past. See if you can remember a situation in which you tried everything you knew how to do and it just was not helping, and then you did something that was different and the situation changed for the better. Ask yourself, what was different about the new way you handled the situation?

It has been our experience that as we describe ecosystemic ideas and the need to do something different in problem situations in the "Making Schools Work" course, students begin to remember problem situations from the past in which they did something different and the problem situation changed for the better. Even before we describe ecosystemic techniques in detail, the students begin to recall unusual ways in which they have solved problems. As the techniques are described or the idea of cooperation is discussed, many students recall having been in a situation in which they felt at their wits' end with a student or parent or colleague, and then, after doing something entirely different in the problem situation, they discovered that things suddenly improved. Although they often report not understanding why things improved, they are able to recognize that they had done something different.

Therapists have noticed a similar phenomenon when working with families. Often parents who bring a child in for therapy have forgotten what they have done and what resources they have drawn on in previous problem situations that have helped them successfully solve their problems. Therefore, a good way for the therapist to begin working with the parents is to help them identify what they have done in the past that has worked.

Consider the example of a child brought to therapy by his parents because they have tried "everything they know" to get the child to do his schoolwork, and he is still not doing the work consistently. One way for the therapist to begin the discussion might be to find out what the parents had done with the older children in the family that had worked and to have them consider those methods as possibilities in the current situation. Which ones might work with this child? How might these methods be modified to fit this particular child in this situation? Another area to examine for earlier successes is what the parents have tried with this child in the past that has worked. What have they done with this child previously to solve either homework problems or some other problem? Are the previously successful responses different than what the parents are doing now? If so, would any of those solutions apply in this situation? The parents might also be asked about what their parents did with them in solving a similar problem. Would any of these strategies work in this situation with their child?

Discussing past successes has several positive effects. Sometimes, after having a discussion about earlier successes, people reapply a solution that has previously worked, and it is once again successful. Another important result of discussing successes can be that people no longer feel as hopeless in the current problem situation. This helps people establish or regain an experimental, creative approach to the problem. Finally, reminiscing about their ability to solve difficult problems in the past can help people generate entirely different new solutions.

Focusing on what people already know how to do has been described in family therapy as a solution orientation (de Shazer, 1985). Developing a similar idea in the area of community organization, Rodale (1987) has contrasted what he calls a capacity-analysis approach with a needs-assessment approach. Rodale points out that most community organizing begins with a needs assessment that focuses on what is lacking in the community. He argues that needs assessments give a clear picture of the weaknesses of a community but provide no understanding of the resources available in the community that can be used to construct solutions to problems. Capacity analysis, on the other hand, searches for the existing skills, strengths, and resources of the community and applies them creatively to "regenerate" the community by using what it has instead of focusing on what it lacks.

Rodale (1987) points out that doing a capacity analysis is fun and provides the immediate reward of feeling hopeful as well as renewing a spirit of creativity and discovery. He writes:

> The needs-oriented approach to learning about a community actually hides a large part of the true nature of any group of people. During needs analysis, much of the capacity so useful to the regeneration of a community remains hidden. Why? Mainly because preoccupation with searching for needs diverts attention from all the local strengths that can be enhanced [p. 20].

Rodale's conception of capacity analysis describes well our assumptions about you. At this point in your personal and professional life, you have solved many problems and have developed numerous skills. You have a personal and professional style that provides you with a useful foundation for finding solutions to chronic problems. It will be helpful if you take the time to assess those things that you do well both in general and in relation to the person or people with whom you have a problem. The ideas we have presented in this book are intended to be used in conjunction with those things you already know how to do. In other words, they are intended to enhance the capacity you already have.

We encourage you to do a capacity analysis of yourself, your classroom, your school, and the community your school serves and then use the ideas in this book to amplify the knowledge and skills that are already available to you.

The following questions might help you begin your personal capacity analysis:

1. What traits do I have that I consider positive? (Examples: I have a good sense of humor. I am loyal, punctual, sensitive, honest.)
2. What skills do I have? (Examples: I vary my teaching techniques. I have a good sense of timing and pacing when I teach. I am well organized.)
3. With what kinds of students do I work well? (Examples: I work well with students who ask for help directly. I work well with bright students who ask lots of questions. I work well with quiet students who have to be drawn out.)
4. In what kinds of situations do I work well? (Examples: I work well in a classroom with lots of give-and-take between the teacher and students. I work well in a structured situation with a specific format for operating.)

Doing a personal capacity analysis might also include assessing what you already know about solving problems. When confronted with a problem situation, ask yourself what you have done that has worked in the past with a similar problem. Would that solution work here? Would some modified form of that solution fit? What have others tried that might work here? What is different about this problem situation that might suggest some modified form of a previously successful solution? What is the situation going to look like when you have solved the problem?

You can combine the general information you have learned

about yourself from your capacity analysis with what you have learned about your problem-solving skills. Consider the following questions:

1. How might I use one of my personal traits or skills to help solve this problem? Could my sense of humor or my ability to be well organized be used to help solve this problem?
2. How could I use my knowledge about the kinds of students I work well with to help solve this problem?
3. How might I combine my knowledge of situations I work well in and past successes to help solve this problem?

This list of questions is not exhaustive. It is intended to help you begin to think about the experience and capacity you already have. You may want to ask yourself a similar series of questions about your students, your school, and the community your school serves in order to help you recognize their respective strengths.

Getting Started and Keeping Going

After we have taught ecosystemic techniques to students in our "Making Schools Work" course, we have them try out techniques of their choice on problems of their choice. As a result of our experience in this course, we recommend that you start small and go slowly.

Start small. Since by definition making a change, even a small one, will affect the entire ecosystem, we recommend selecting a small problem to start with and making as small a change as possible in relation to the problem. For example, you may have several problems in your classroom that you would like to tackle. Choose the one that will be the easiest for you to work on, or if you have several students in a class who cause problems, choose only one of them to start with.

Go slowly. After selecting one problem that is the easiest for you to start with, select a technique that interests you and use it. Then wait. Look for changes. Look for changes in the problem situation with the problem person; look for changes in others in the classroom; notice any change in attitude on your part. Give the change you have initiated some time to work. In our experience, you are more likely to encounter difficulties if you try to move too quickly than if you move too slowly.

Develop a Plan. Education has been described as a lonely profession. Isolation and lack of support take their toll on even the most dedicated among us. We have found that the people who have most consistently used ecosystemic techniques are those who have found ways to keep introducing and reintroducing ecosystemic ideas into their daily routines.

As you might imagine, the methods various individuals have used to encourage themselves to remember and use ecosystemic ideas are quite varied. Teachers have compiled a library of articles and anecdotes; made deliberate attempts to find the humor in difficult situations; taught ecosystemic ideas to their students; kept a log or journal; made tapes describing particularly memorable incidents involving ecosystemic ideas, to be played back when it seemed appropriate; put a container on their desk labeled "ecosystemic methods" and dropped a marble in it each time they used an ecosystemic technique; made up note cards outlining various ecosystemic techniques and kept the cards close at hand; made signs such as "Don't Frame Them—Reframe Yourself" and posted them around the room; made a poster showing a thumb (the problem) blotting out the sun (everything else); put the words *reframe, positive connotation,* and so on on the classroom wall calendar so that each month a new reminder appeared; put predictable problems on a poster with a reframing for each; and listened for negative descriptions of the problem person from others and then practiced positive connotation using those negative descriptions as points of departure. Teachers have even made fortune cookies with ecosystemic messages in them.

Involve Others as Consultants to Encourage Your Creativity. Each of the various ways that people have found to remind themselves how to use ecosystemic ideas are ways of changing at a time when things are stuck.

One of the best ways to keep yourself involved with ecosystemic ideas is to form a consultation group. The purpose of consultation groups is to enable a group of people interested in ecosystemic ideas to share their experiences and help each other find creative ways of being different in problem situations. When a group of educators shares ideas and thinks of creative ways of being different in problem situations, the successes of one can positively influence every group member. In practice, these groups have the potential for amplifying the small changes made in one classroom and influencing the entire ecosystem of the school.

Therapists also find it necessary at times to find ways to encourage themselves to think creatively and not get into a rut when working with clients. De Shazer and Molnar (1984b) have discussed the need to introduce what they call "random" elements into a social system to encourage creativity and promote change. Obviously, an individual can find ways to encourage his or her creativity and help her- or himself to do something different in problem situations. However, the process is made easier if you have the support of at least one other person. In much the same way that it is necessary for both of our eyes to function in order to have depth perception, having at least one other different (but sympathetic) view of a problem situation provides a more complete and perhaps more useful picture. Also, other people are an excellent source of the random comments, behaviors, and points of view that often lead to creative solutions. A good many solutions have been the result of someone trying to figure out the meaning or significance of something apparently unrelated to the problem at hand.

In their article "Changing Teams/Changing Families," de Shazer and Molnar (1984a) describe how a three-person therapy team (one therapist in the room with the clients and two observing from behind a one-way mirror) were helped to find a creative solution in a difficult case by the random comment of a colleague.

During the third therapy session with a divorced couple and their teenaged daughter, a therapist who was not involved in the case entered the room where the two therapists were observing the session from behind the one-way mirror. On entering the room, the therapist glanced at the family and commented that the father resembled Paladin in the old television series "Have Gun, Will Travel." She then left the room.

The two therapists who were part of the therapy team

working on the case began discussing just how much the man did look like Paladin. Subsequently, the team used the random comment of their colleague to design an intervention to assist the parents with their parenting problem. They commented to the family about the father's resemblance to Paladin and then

> suggested that perhaps the best way for him to be a father would be to have his daughter move back in with her mother (which mother wanted) but remain on call—"Have Discipline, Will Travel"—should his former wife need his assistance. This frame was accepted by both Mr. Y. and his former wife and used by them to establish (for the first time) a cooperative relationship in raising their daughter [p. 484].

In the preceding case example, the parents initially regarded raising their daughter as an either-or proposition: either the father was responsible for raising the girl, or the mother was. This is very similar to the either-or perspectives often adopted by educators in problem situations. It is common for educators having difficulty with a student, a colleague, or a parent to understand the situation as one in which either there is something wrong with the other person, or they are incompetent. Another common either-or perspective is that either the problem person must change, or I must. Such either-or perspectives make cooperation difficult, encourage negative rather than positive descriptions of the problem, and stifle creativity.

If, like the therapists in our example, you can establish a group that understands ecosystemic ideas, the group will support and encourage your creativity. A consultation group will help you to avoid the perceptual trap of either-or thinking and make it possible to turn even random comments into useful resources for promoting positive change. Educators who have taken our "Making Schools Work" course have recognized the importance of group support. Perhaps that is why so many have taught ecosystemic ideas to their co-workers, students, teacher aides, and even school secretaries and custodians.

What We Have Learned from Our Students

When we teach the "Making Schools Work" course, we most often teach it during three weekends with about a month between sessions. Over the years, we have noticed certain similarities in the approach our students take to our ideas. Understanding the rhythm of their development in using ecosystemic ideas may help you learn how to build on successes and overcome setbacks as you try these ideas.

During the first weekend, our students tend to be skeptical and to regard reframing (the first technique we teach them) as a gimmick. They indulge us, however, and agree to try reframing in a chronic problem situation in which they are willing to risk doing something different. Although students select a wide variety of problems to work on, we always urge them to think small and to make the smallest change possible.

When the students return for the second weekend, most of their previous skepticism is replaced by puzzlement. How does reframing work? In our experience, about 80 percent of the students who tried reframing between class sessions have either successfully changed the problem situation in which they used it or have made progress toward solving their problem. During the second weekend, instead of facing skeptical students, we face nervous students who do not know what to do next and who are afraid that a single misstep might result in the return of their problem. Therefore, the first thing we teach them about in this session is predicting a relapse (Chapter Ten). We tell them to adopt an altogether natural attitude toward the change, that is, to be mildly skeptical toward and somewhat puzzled by it. We explain to them that a relapse would be normal and predictable and tell them to say so to the person with whom they had the problem, if it seems appropriate. We suggest that they behave almost any way they wish as long as they do not behave the way they used to in the problem situation. After having thus reassured our students, we proceed to teach them positive connotation of motive and function and symptom prescription. By the end of the second weekend, some students have decided that, far from being simpleminded tricks, ecosystemic techniques are almost mystical in their power.

When our students return for the final weekend, most have had continued success using ecosystemic ideas. However, as a result of more experience with the ideas, they tend to regard them as neither tricks nor mystical mechanisms for producing change as if by magic. By this point, most students have discovered that they can use ecosystemic ideas quite comfortably in conjunction with their style and the demands of their particular circumstances. Our students also begin to realize that all of the ecosystemic techniques we have taught them are ways of changing themselves. It is at this point that students are most interested in finding ways to make sure that ecosystemic ideas stay with them once the course is over. They like the changes they have made.

It was working with students who had reached this point that enabled us to understand the essential elements of getting started and keeping going that we have described in this chapter. We hope that reading *Changing Problem Behavior in Schools* will encourage you to try ecosystemic ideas and to find ways of integrating them effectively into your personal style, just as participating in the "Making Schools Work" course has encouraged our students to do. We wish you well.

Resource:
Practicing Behavior
Change Strategies

We have provided the activities in this section as resources to help you use our ideas in your school or classroom. Each ecosystemic technique described in Part Two has a practice activity in this section. The practice activity for each ecosystemic technique takes you through a step-by-step process that will help you use that technique with a problem you have selected. Doing these practice activities will also help you to clarify which of the ecosystemic techniques is most appropriate for your problem.

The practice activities in this section may be reproduced without the prior permission of Jossey-Bass. Please feel free to make copies of any or all the activities for your use.

Practice Activity: Reframing

Think of a problem you are currently having. Usually problems have names and faces. Think of a real situation with real people that is currently a problem for you. Jot down some notes for yourself.

1. Describe what happens in the problem situation in specific behavioral terms. Who does what? When do they do it? Who else is involved?

2. How do you usually respond to the problem behavior, and what is the usual result?

3. What is your current explanation of why the person behaves this way?

4. What positive alternative explanations might there be for this behavior?

5. Based on one of your positive alternative explanations of the person's behavior, how could you respond differently than you have previously? What might you actually say or do based on one of these alternative explanations?

Practice Activity: Positive Connotation of Motive

Think of a problem you are currently having. Jot down some notes for yourself about the problem. Be as specific as possible.

1. What does the person do? When do they do it? Who else is involved?

2. How do you usually respond and what result do you get?

3. Why do you think the person does this? What do you think the person's motives are for this behavior?

4. What positive motives might there be for this behavior?

5. Based on one or more of these positive motives for the person's behavior, how might you respond differently than you have in the past? What might you actually say or do based on one of these positive motives?

Practice Activity: Positive Connotation of Function

Think of a problem you are currently having. Jot down some notes for yourself about the problem. Be as specific as possible in describing the problem behavior.

1. Who does what, when, to whom, and so on?

2. How do you usually respond, and what result do you get?

3. What are some of the functions of this behavior that you presently see?

4. What are some positive ecosystemic functions of this behavior? (Remember, a function is not necessarily an intended result. A function is a factor related to or dependent on other factors. If *A* happens, so do *B, C,* and *D.*)

5. Based on one or more of these positive ecosystemic functions, how could you respond differently than you have in the past? What might you actually say or do based on one of these positive functions?

Practice Activity: Symptom Prescription

Think of a problem you are currently having. Jot down some notes for yourself about the problem. Be as specific as possible in describing the problematic behavior.

1. Who does what, when, to whom, and so on?

2. How do you usually respond to get the person to stop the behavior? What result do you usually get?

3. What are some ways the behavior could be performed differently, for example, at a different time or place, in a different way, or for a different reason?

4. How might you request that the person perform the modified behavior so that it can be regarded in a positive way?

Practice Activity: Storming the Back Door

Think of a person (or group) whose behavior is currently a problem for you. Jot down some notes for yourself.

1. Describe the nonproblem behaviors or attributes of a person (or group) whose behavior is a problem for you.

2. List situations in which a behavior of the problem person is not a problem for you.

3. Select an item from the ones you have listed above that would be the easiest for you to comment on positively and genuinely.

4. Based on the item you have selected, what might you say to the person whose behavior is a problem for you? In what situation will you say it?

Practice Activity: Locating Exceptions

Think of a person whose behavior is currently a problem for you. Jot down your responses to the following:

1. List the situations in which the person you have identified does not exhibit the behavior that concerns you.

2. Note any differences you can identify between the problem and nonproblem situations.

3. List the behaviors, qualities, and characteristics of the person you have identified that you do not want to change.

4. Identify what you are already doing that works in relation to this person. How are you different in nonproblem situations?

5. Write down a plan for using what you have learned by responding to 1 through 4 above in order to increase the amount of time devoted to nonproblem behavior(s).

References

Amatea, E. S., and Fabrick, F. "Family Systems Counseling: A Positive Alternative to Traditional Counseling." *Elementary School Guidance and Counseling*, 1981, *15* (3), 223-237.

Anderson, C. "An Ecological Developmental Model for Family Orientation in School Psychology." *Journal of School Psychology*, 1983, *21* (3), 179-189.

Aponte, H. J. "The Family-School Interview: An Eco-Structural Approach." *Family Process*, 1976, *15* (3), 303-311.

Asimov. I. *Foundation's Edge*. New York: Ballantine Books, 1982.

Bateson, G. *Steps to an Ecology of Mind*. New York: Chandler, 1972.

Bateson, G. *Mind and Nature: A Necessary Unity*. New York: Dutton, 1979.

Beck, A. T. *Depression: Clinical, Experimental and Theoretical Aspects*. New York: Harper & Row, 1967.

Bercuvitz, J. "Greenfield, Iowa: America's Number-One Regeneration Town." *Regeneration*, 1987, *3* (1), 1, 4.

Berger, M. "Special Education Programs." In M. Berger, G. J. Jurkovic, and Associates (eds.), *Practicing Family Therapy in Diverse Settings: New Approaches to the Connections Among Families, Therapists, and Treatment Settings*. San Francisco: Jossey-Bass, 1984.

Bernard, C. P., and Corrales, R. G. *The Theory and Technique of Family Therapy*. Springfield, Ill.: Thomas, 1979.

Bertalanffy, L. von. "General System Theory and Psychiatry." In

S. Arieti (ed.), *American Handbook of Psychiatry.* New York: Basic Books, 1966.

Bogdan, J. L. "Paradoxical Communication as Interpersonal Influence." *Family Process,* 1982, *21* (4), 443-452.

Bogdan, J. L. "Family Organization as an Ecology of Ideas: An Alternative to the Reification of Family Systems." *Family Process,* 1984, *23,* 375-388.

Bogdan, J. L. "Do Families Really Need Problems?" *Family Therapy Networker,* 1986, *10* (4), 30-35, 67-69.

Bogdan, J. L. "Epistemology as a Semantic Pollutant." *Journal of Marital and Family Therapy,* 1987, *13* (1), 27-36.

Bowman, P., and Goldberg, M. " 'Reframing': A Tool for the School Psychologist." *Psychology in the Schools,* 1983, *20* (4), 210-214.

Chambless, D. L., and Goldstein, H. J. "Behavioral Psychotherapy." In R. Corsini (ed.), *Current Psychotherapies.* Itasca, Ill.: Peacock, 1979.

Coles, R. *Children of Crisis: A Study of Courage and Fear.* Boston: Little, Brown, 1967.

Coles, R. *Migrants, Sharecroppers, Mountaineers.* Boston: Little, Brown, 1971a.

Coles, R. *The South Goes North.* Boston: Little, Brown, 1971b.

Coles, R. *Eskimos, Chicanos, Indians.* Boston: Little, Brown, 1977a.

Coles, R. *Privileged Ones: The Well Off and Rich in America.* Boston: Little, Brown, 1977b.

de Lone, R. *Small Futures: Children, Inequality, and the Limits of Liberal Reform.* San Diego, Calif.: Harcourt Brace Jovanovich, 1979.

de Shazer, S. *Patterns of Brief Family Therapy: An Ecosystemic Approach.* New York: Guilford Press, 1982.

de Shazer, S. *Keys to Solution.* New York: Norton, 1985.

de Shazer, S., and Molnar, A. "Changing Teams/Changing Families." *Family Process,* 1984a, *23* (4), 481-486.

de Shazer, S., and Molnar, A. "Four Useful Interventions in Brief Family Therapy." *Journal of Marital and Family Therapy,* 1984b, *10* (3), 297-304.

de Shazer, S., and others. "Brief Therapy: Focused Solution Development." *Family Process,* 1986, *25,* 207-221.

DiCocco, B. E. "A Guide to Family/School Interventions for the Family Therapist." *Contemporary Family Therapy*, 1986, *8* (1), 50-61.

Dreikurs, R. *Psychology in the Classroom: A Manual for Teachers.* New York: Harper & Row, 1968.

Duhl, B. S., and Duhl, F. J. "Integrative Family Therapy." In A. S. Gurman and D. P. Kniskern (eds.), *Handbook of Family Therapy.* New York: Brunner/Mazel, 1981.

Ellis, A. *Reason and Emotion in Psychotherapy.* New York: Lyle Stuart, 1962.

Ergenziner, E. "Sich die Arbeit leichter machen" [To make your work easier]. In C. Hennig and U. Knödler, *Problem-Schüler Problem-Familien* [Problem students, problem families]. Basel, Switzerland: Belz Verlag, 1985.

Fay, A. *Making Things Better by Making Them Worse.* New York: Hawthorne Books, 1978.

Festinger, L. *A Theory of Cognitive Dissonance.* Stanford, Calif.: Stanford University Press, 1957.

Fine, M. J., and Holt, P. "Intervening with School Problems: A Family Systems Perspective." *Psychology in the Schools*, 1983, *20* (1), 59-66.

Fish, M. C., and Shashi, J. "A Systems Approach in Working with Learning Disabled Children: Implications for the School." *Journal of Learning Disabilities*, 1985, *18* (10), 592-595.

Foster, M. A. "Schools." In M. Berger, G. J. Jurkovic, and Associates (eds.), *Practicing Family Therapy in Diverse Settings: New Approaches to the Connections Among Families, Therapists, and Treatment Settings.* San Francisco: Jossey-Bass, 1984.

Frykman, J. *The Hassle Handbook.* Berkeley, Calif.: Regent Street Books, 1984.

Golden, L. "Brief Family Interventions in a School Setting." *Elementary School Guidance and Counseling*, 1983, *17* (4), 288-293.

Gould, S. J. *Ever Since Darwin: Reflections in Natural History.* New York: Norton, 1977.

Gould, S. J. *The Panda's Thumb: More Reflections in Natural History.* New York: Norton, 1982.

Grau, U., Möller, J., and Gunnarsson, J. I. "Reframing von

Problemsituationen Oder: Probleme einmal anders angepackt."
Sportpsychologie, January 1987, 27-30.

Greenberg, R. P. "Anti-Expectation Techniques in Psychotherapy:
The Power of Negative Thinking." *Psychotherapy: Theory,
Research and Practice,* 1973, *10* (2), 145-148.

Haley, J. *Uncommon Therapy.* New York: Norton, 1973.

Haley, J. *Problem Solving Therapy.* New York: Harper & Row,
1978.

Hannafin, M. J., and Witt, J. C. "System Intervention and the
School Psychologist: Maximizing Interplay Among Roles and
Functions." *Professional Psychology: Research and Practice,*
1983, *14* (1), 128-136.

Hansen, J. C. (ed.). *Family Therapy with School Related Problems.*
Rockville, Md.: Aspen, 1984.

Hawkins, R. P., Peterson, R. F., Schweid, E., and Bijou, S. W.
"Behavior Therapy in the Home: Amelioration of Problem
Parent-Child Relations with the Parent in a Therapeutic Role."
In J. Haley (ed.), *Changing Families.* Orlando, Fla.: Grune &
Stratton, 1971.

Hoban, R. *Bread and Jam for Frances.* New York: Harper & Row,
1964.

Howard, J. *System Intervention and School Psychology.* Paper
presented at the fourth International Colloquium in School
Psychology, Jerusalem, July 1980.

Huslage, S., and Stein, J. "A Systems Approach for the Child Study
Team." *Social Work in Education,* 1985, *7* (2), 114-123.

Jaynes, J. H., and Rugg, C. A. *Adolescents, Alcohol and Drugs: A
Practical Guide for Those Who Work with Young People.*
Springfield, Ill.: Thomas, 1988.

Johnston, J. C., and Fields, P. H. "School Consultation with the
'Classroom Family.'" *School Counselor,* 1981, *29* (2), 140-146.

Kohl, J., and Kohl, H. *The View from the Oak: The Private Worlds
of Other Creatures.* San Francisco: Sierra Club Books, 1977.

Kral, R. "Indirect Therapy in the Schools." In S. de Shazer and R.
Kral (eds.), *Indirect Approaches in Therapy.* Rockville, Md.:
Aspen, 1986.

Lindquist, B., Molnar, A., and Brauckmann, L. "Working with

School Related Problems Without Going to School." *Journal of Strategic and Systemic Therapies*, 1987, *6* (4), 44–50.

Lovelock, J., and Margulis, L. Interview in *Gaia: Goddess of the Earth*. NOVA publication no. 1302. Transcript of a Public Broadcasting Service presentation, January 28, 1986. Produced by WGBH, Boston.

McDaniel, S. H. "Treating School Problems in Family Therapy." *Elementary School Guidance and Counseling*, 1981, *15* (3), 214–236.

Maher, C. A. "Intervention with School Social Systems: A Behavioral-Systems Approach." *School Psychology Review*, 1981, *10* (4), 449–508.

Mahoney, M. J. *Cognition and Behavior Modification*. Cambridge, Mass.: Ballinger, 1974.

Mandel, H. P., and others. "Reaching Emotionally Disturbed Children: 'Judo' Principles in Remedial Education." *American Journal of Orthopsychiatry*, 1975, *45* (5), 867–874.

Meichenbaum, D. *Cognitive-Behavior Modification*. New York: Plenum Press, 1977.

Miller, W. R. *Living as If: How Positive Faith Can Change Your Life*. Philadelphia: Westminster Press, 1985.

Minuchin, S. *Families and Family Therapy*. Cambridge, Mass.: Harvard University Press, 1974.

Molnar, A. "A Systemic Perspective on Solving Problems in the School." *NASSP Bulletin*, 1986, *70* (493), 32–40.

Molnar, A., and de Shazer, S. "Solution-Focused Therapy: Toward the Identification of Therapeutic Tasks." *Journal of Marital and Family Therapy*, 1987, *13* (4), 349–358.

Molnar, A., and Lindquist, B. *A Systemic Approach to Increasing School Effectiveness*. Paper presented at the national conference of the Association for Supervision and Curriculum Development, Anaheim, California, March 1982.

Molnar, A., and Lindquist, B. "Demons or Angels? A Lot Depends on How You Respond to Misbehavior." *Learning*, 1984a, *13* (4), 22–26.

Molnar, A., and Lindquist, B. "Erkenntnisse über Verhalten und Strukturen verbinden: Ein systemisches Ansatz, die Leistungsfähigkeit der Schule zu erhohen" [Knowledge about the relationship between behavior and structure: A systemic approach to increasing school effectiveness]. *Zeitschrift für Systemische Therapie*, 1984b, *2* (5), 2-16.

Molnar, A., and Lindquist, B. "Increasing School Effectiveness." Association of Wisconsin School Administrators, *Update*, May 1985, 6-8.

Molnar, A., and Lindquist, B. *An Uncommon Approach to Motivation and Discipline Problems*. Paper presented at the national conference of the Association for Supervision and Curriculum Development, Boston, March 1988.

Molnar, A., Lindquist, B., and Hage, K. "Von der Möglichkeit der Veränderung problematischer Unterrichtssituationen: Unterricht als selbstreferentielles System" [The possibility of changing problematic teaching situations: Instruction as a self-referencing system]. *Zeitschrift für systemische Therapie*, 1985, *3* (4), 216-223.

Nisbett, R. E., and Ross, L. D. *Human Inference: Strategies and Shortcomings of Social Judgment*. Englewood Cliffs, N.J.: Prentice-Hall, 1980.

Okun, B. (ed.). *Family Therapy with School Related Problems*. Rockville, Md.: Aspen, 1984.

Patterson, G. R. *Families: Applications of Social Learning to Family Life*. Champaign, Ill.: Research Press, 1971.

Pfeiffer, S. I., and Tittler, B. I. "Utilizing the Multidisciplinary Team to Facilitate a School-Family Systems Orientation." *School Psychology Review*, 1983, *12* (2), 168-173.

Power, T. J., and Bartholomew, K. L. "Getting Unstuck in the Middle: A Case Study in Family–School System Consultation." *School Psychology Review*, 1985, *14* (2), 222-229.

Random House Dictionary of the English Language. New York: Random House, 1971, 1046.

Rodale, R. "Breaking New Ground: The Search for Sustainable Agriculture." *Futurist*, 1983, *17* (1), 15-20.

Rodale, R. *Hopeful Living: How to Put Regeneration to Work in Your Life*. Emmaus, Pa.: Rodale Press, 1987.

Rosenthal, R., and Jacobson, L. *Pygmalion in the Classroom: Teacher Expectation and Pupils' Intellectual Development*. New York: Holt, Rinehart & Winston, 1968.

Rubin, L. B. *Worlds of Pain: Life in the Working Class Family.* New York: Basic Books, 1976.

Seltzer, L. F. *Paradoxical Strategies in Psychotherapy: A Comprehensive Overview and Guidebook.* New York: Wiley, 1986.

Skinner, B. F. *The Technology of Teaching.* East Norwalk, Conn.: Appleton-Century-Crofts, 1968.

Smith, A. H., Jr. "Encountering the Family System in School-Related Behavior Problems." *Psychology in the Schools,* 1978, *15* (3), 379-386.

Stuart, R. B. "Operant Interpersonal Treatment for Marital Discord." *Journal of Consulting and Clinical Psychology,* 1969, *33,* 675-682.

Taylor, S. E., and Brown, J. D. "Illusion and Well-Being: A Social Psychological Perspective on Mental Health." *Psychological Bulletin,* 1988, *103* (2), 193-210.

Tucker, B. Z., and Dyson, E. "The Family and the School: Utilizing Human Resources to Promote Learning." *Family Process,* 1976, *15* (1), 125-141.

Watzlawick, P., Weakland, J., and Fisch, R. *Change: Principles of Problem Formation and Problem Resolution.* New York: Norton, 1974.

Weeks, G. R. (ed.). *Promoting Change Through Paradoxical Therapy.* Homewood, Ill.: Dow Jones-Irwin, 1985.

Weeks, G. R., and L'Abate, L. *Paradoxical Psychotherapy: Theory and Practice with Individuals, Couples and Families.* New York: Brunner/Mazel, 1982.

Wendt, R. N., and Zake, J. "Family Systems Theory and School Psychology: Implications for Training and Practice." *Psychology in the Schools,* 1984, *21,* 204-210.

Whitaker, C. A. "Psychotherapy of the Absurd: With Special Emphasis on the Psychotherapy of Aggression." *Family Process,* 1975, *14* (1), 1-16.

Wielkiewicz, R. M. *Behavior Management in the Schools.* Elmsford, N.Y.: Pergamon Press, 1986.

Williams, J. M., and Weeks, G. R. "Use of Paradoxical Techniques in a School Setting." *American Journal of Family Therapy,* 1984, *12* (3), 47-57.

Wlodkowski, R. J. *Enhancing Adult Motivation to Learn: A Guide*

to Improving Instruction and Increasing Learner Achievement.
San Francisco: Jossey-Bass, 1986a.

Wlodkowski, R. J. *Motivation and Teaching: A Practical Guide.*
Washington, D.C.: National Education Association, 1986b.

Worden, M. "Classroom Behavior as a Function of the Family
System." *School Counselor,* 1981, *28* (3), 178–188.

Index